The Arno Press Cinema Program

CRITICAL APPROACHES TO
FEDERICO FELLINI'S
"8½"

Albert Edward Benderson

ARNO PRESS
A NEW YORK TIMES COMPANY
New York • 1974

This volume was selected for the
Dissertations on Film Series
of the ARNO PRESS CINEMA PROGRAM
by Garth S. Jowett, Carleton University

First publication in book form, Arno Press, 1974

THE ARNO PRESS CINEMA PROGRAM
For complete listing of cinema titles see last pages

Manufactured in the United States of America

— — — — — — — — — — — — — — — — —

Library of Congress Cataloging in Publication Data

Benderson, Albert Edward.
    Critical approaches to Federico Fellini's "8 1/2."

    (The Arno Press cinema program) (Dissertations on
film series)
    1. Otto e mezzo (Motion picture) 2. Fellini,
Federico. I. Title. II. Series. III. Series:
Dissertations on film series.
PN1997.O77B4   791.43'0233'0924   74-2078
ISBN 0-405-04877-7

CRITICAL APPROACHES TO FEDERICO FELLINI'S **8-1/2**

by

Albert Edward Benderson

A dissertation submitted to the
Faculty of the Graduate School of State
University of New York at Buffalo in partial
fulfillment of the requirements for the degree of
Doctor of Philosophy

June 1973

ACKNOWLEDGEMENTS

I would like to thank Dr. Gerald O'Grady without whose
guidance, insight, encouragement and faith this dissertation
would never have been completed. I would also like to thank
Dr. Neil Schmitz and Dr. Stefan Fleischer for their assist-
ance in the editing of this paper. Furthermore, the libraries
at the Museum of Modern Art and Lincoln Center; the Elgin,
Thalia, and New Yorker Theaters; and Cinemabilia were all
invaluable sources of basic research material.

TABLE OF CONTENTS

CHAPTER I

INTRODUCTION

In the Winter/Spring 1972 issue of Sight and Sound, an
international poll of film critics resulted in 8-1/2 being
ranked fourth among the top ten films of all time.[1] Although
the validity of such polls remains dubious at best, the ele-
vation of Fellini's masterpiece to such an exalted position
in the film pantheon just a decade after its release reflects
its soaring international reputation as one of the great
works of film art.

Yet, as is the case with so many other great films,
8-1/2 has not yet received the detailed interpretative attention a work of its magnitude deserves. While a literary work
of similar magnitude would have volumes of intensive explica-
tion devoted to it, 8-1/2 remains largely untouched by
detailed critical analysis. It has only been dealt with in
short articles in film journals or brief chapters in books,
neither of which afford sufficient space to develop a comprehensive, in-depth interpretation of the film.

The following paper is intended to provide just such an

[1]"Top Ten 72," Sight and Sound, 41 (Winter 1971/72), 12.

intensive critical examination of the film. The primary
objective is to present a comprehensive close reading of
8-1/2, focusing upon the manner in which film technique gives
rise to meaning. Thus, the first section is devoted to a
close reading of 8-1/2 in the New Critical mode, focusing
upon what Ted Perry has called its "intra-referential context."[2] This is the context created in a film by the interaction of its spatial and temporal elements, including photography, sound, visual composition, lighting, and editing.
This is a context of meaning which arises from within the
film itself, rather than being imposed upon it from an outside, foreign source.

This contextual approach is particularly rewarding when
applied to 8-1/2, because the film is a tightly organized and
highly unified work of art. Every element of the film contributes to the meaning of the whole. Moreover, 8-1/2 is a
film of great subtlety and complexity. This complexity
arises, in large part, from its first-person narrative style.
The film draws us into the mind of Guido, its protagonist, as
it flows freely from present realities into an interior world
rich in dreams, fantasies, hypnagogic visions, hallucinations, and other mental apparitions which arise from the
depths of the unconscious. The film, in fact, is structured

[2]Ted Perry, "A Contextual Study of M. Antonioni's Film
L'Eclisse," Speech Monographs, 37, No. 2 (June 1970), 81.

by the flow of Guido's consciousness, much in the manner of
first-person narratives in literature. Thus, the first section of this paper deals in considerable detail with the manner in which Fellini structures this flow of consciousness as
viewed from a contextual perspective.

While the New Critical method of analysis is the necessary first step in approaching a work of art, it often suggests other useful critical modes. In the case of 8-1/2, the
contextual perspective reveals that the images which arise in
Guido's thoughts and fantasies, as they are portrayed upon
the screen, are clearly archetypal. A consistent pattern of
images explicitly evocative of archetypes such as the anima
and the mandala create a Jungian context from which the film
can also be viewed. The evidence within the film for an
archetypal reading is so compelling that it can in no sense
be argued that it is imposed from without.

The film may be viewed from a Jungian perspective in
terms of its theme as well. As in many of Fellini's other
films, the central theme of 8-1/2 is one of self-realization,
a process which in Guido's case entails a confrontation with
his archetypal projections, thus conforming to that process
of human development which Jung calls individuation. Violet
S. de Laszlo describes individuation as ". . . the process of
becoming the independent personality who is (relatively) free
from the domination of parental archetypes and independent of
supportive structures of the social environment." She adds

that the person who achieves this state of individuation can
". . . establish his own individual values and relationships
because they are based on the reality of his self-knowledge
and not on a system of illusions and rationalizations."[3]

Fellini uses much the same language when he describes
the central theme of many of his films:

> . . . In 3 or 4 of my films, what is constantly
> repeated is the attempt to suggest to man the process of
> individual liberation--that is, to trace one's steps to
> see where certain dents, certain illnesses started,
> where the psychological cancers were formed. In going
> back personally, individually, as a most private artist
> reflecting on my walk of life, I seem to recognize a
> certain conditioning of a pedagogical nature, of an
> education that made me suffer, which obstructed me, made
> me stop. My presumptuous nature leads me to think that
> it would be worthwile and just to try to do in my films--
> as an artist does in his books or another artist in the
> form more congenial to him--to try to identify what his
> educational conditioning was, in order to attempt to
> conquer it, to make it harmless so that the error may
> not be repeated. I want to suggest to modern man a road
> of inner liberation, to accept and love life the way it
> is without idealizing it, without creating concepts
> about it, without projecting oneself into idealized
> images on a moral or ethical plane. I want to try to
> give back to man a virginal availability, his innocence
> as he had in childhood, but knowing this. . . .
> Here then--8-1/2, Giulietta Degli Spiriti, and even
> La Dolci Vita tried to propose this backward walk, try-
> ing to identify this pathological conditioning. What
> are the myths that must be destroyed? . . . Well, the
> ideals, the ideals in general. I think that the ideal,
> the idealized life, the idealized concepts can be
> extremely dangerous for our mental health, and it is
> what I try to express in my films. . . .[4]

[3]Violet S. de Laszlo, "Introduction," Psyche and Symbol
by C. G. Jung (Garden City, 1958), p. xxix.

[4]Iriving Levine, "I Was Born for the Cinema--a Conversation with Federico Fellini," Film Comment (Fall 1966), 80-81.

In 8-1/2 Guido struggles to liberate himself from a number of idealized concepts. He struggles, for instance, to rid himself of the guilt which arises from flaunting the Church's idealized and anachronistic moral values. More deeply, perhaps, he struggles to liberate himself from the domination of idealized archetypes, specifically the anima, which alienate him from the world.

Given the central role of this archetypal theme in 8-1/2, the second section of the paper will deal with the film as viewed from a Jungian perspective. This archetypal approach will remain consistent with the essentially contextual methodology of the dissertation. When Fellini creates images and deals with themes which are unmistakably archetypal in character, the archetypal reference will be examined only to the extent that it relates directly to the meaning of the film.

In the third section the excesses of certain critics who do not adhere to this fundamental principle of contextual analysis shall be dealt with. Specifically, the popular but erroneous notion that 8-1/2 is Fellini's autobiography will be examined. In its most extreme form this assumption leads certain writers to suggest that Guido is, in fact, the author of 8-1/2. While this is rather appealing and cute, not to mention chic, it totally misrepresents the film and rests upon certain preconceptions which cannot be justified in terms of the context of the film.

The fourth section of the dissertation will suggest a more responsible approach towards viewing the relationship between the director and his film by placing 8-1/2 in the context of Fellini's work. It will demonstrate that 8-1/2 deals with certain themes and motifs which recur and reverberate throughout Fellini's films.

Thus, the dissertation comprises an attempt to view Fellini's 8-1/2 from four different critical perspectives. The validity of the third perspective is challenged, while the others are shown to be useful and rewarding vantage points from which to explore this great masterpiece of the cinema.

CHAPTER II

8-1/2--A CONTEXTUAL ANALYSIS

I. THE FIRST-PERSON NARRATIVE

If one were to use a literary analogy, something one should always be hesitant to do when dealing with films, he would be quite accurate in saying that 8-1/2 is presented in the cinematic equivalent of the first-person narrative mode. Clearly, the entire film unfolds from Guido's point of view. In fact, Guido appears in every scene of the film, so that we only see what he himself is able to perceive. Usually, we are allowed to know only what Guido knows about the events which surround him. When his wife, for instance, mysteriously becomes angry with him after their pleasant reunion at the spa, we share Guido's puzzlement as to the cause for her sudden change of temperament. It is only when she tells him that, upon arriving at the spa, she spotted Guido's mistress, that we learn, along with Guido, the cause of her anger. Thus, rather than provide us with a scene in which Luisa spots Carla before meeting Guido, Fellini makes Guido's presence a prerequisite for every scene in the film. We see only what Guido himself sees, and share his puzzlement and consternation when events outside his, and our, immediate

7

perception, such as Luisa's glimpse of Carla, impinge upon his life.

Guido's presence, in fact, dominates and structures the entire film to the extent that he is really the only major character in the film. None of the other characters are of even comparable importance. Even those who play the greatest role in his life, Luisa, Carla, and Claudia, appear in only a relatively few scenes. They move in and out of his life in an almost episodic manner.

The fact that Guido plays the central role in every scene of the film is only one of the myriad devices which Fellini uses to identify the viewpoint of the film with that of Guido's mind. The most striking device, perhaps, consists of those shots which are photographed as if the camera were literally inside Guido's head. From the opening scene, these first-person shots pervade the entire film. When Guido floats above the beach in this introductory nightmare, for instance, the camera looks down from his vantage point as he frantically attempts to free himself from the rope tied to his ankle and held by a man below. As Suzanne Budgen puts it:

> Then when Guido is being hauled down from the sky we get a sight of his foot from above and then of his hand trying to free it, as if they were our own, and this leads us from the feeling of closeness to the feeling of actual identity.[1]

[1] Suzanne Budgen, Fellini (England, 1966), pp. 55-56.

Of course, in this scene the camera is inside Guido's head in more than one sense. Not only is this particular shot photographed from his vantage point above the beach, but also the entire sequence is part of a nightmare which Guido is dreaming, so that we are also inside his head in the sense that we share his dream. Simultaneously, we are inside the heads of both Guido, the dreamer, and Guido, the character within the dream.

There are, of course, other examples of shots in which the camera seems to move directly into Guido's head. For instance, when Guido discusses his script with the Cardinal's lay assistant while walking through the garden, the subjective camera dollies through the woods in Guido's place. When the lay assistant enters the frame, he gazes directly into the camera as he speaks to Guido, thus reinforcing our sense that the camera has moved inside Guido's head.

This technique of having characters talk directly into the camera as they speak to Guido, incidently, is a frequently used technique throughout the film and often serves to reinforce our feeling that, at times, the camera has moved inside Guido's head and is showing us precisely what he, himself, sees. When Daumier talks to Guido about his script in the garden of the spa, we find an example of just such a shot, for he looks directly into the camera as he speaks to Guido while walking beside him.

In the scene in which Guido fantasizes an audience with the Cardinal in the steam baths beneath the spa, we have an

even more complex example of this type of subjective shot.
After Guido hurries out of the steam room to meet the Cardinal, the film cuts to an intricate traveling shot in which
the camera moves through the underground corridors as if it
were mounted upon Guido's shoulders, while various associates
of his rush towards him with items of clothing for him to put
on. Since we are now looking through Guido's eyes, his associates seem to place the clothes in unseen hands underneath
the camera and to speak directly into the lens as they implore
Guido to ask the Cardinal for various special favors. Once
again, because this scene is fantasized by Guido, we are in
his head in the double sense of both seeing through the eyes
of Guido, as he is personified in the daydream, and experiencing the fantasy itself, as it arises in Guido's mind.

There are also a number of shots of shorter duration,
scattered throughout the film, in which the point of view of
the camera is identical to that of the protagonist. For
instance, there is a brief first-person shot in Guido's
graveyard dream, when the camera, presumably in his place,
chases his father through the entrance of his tomb. Another
instance occurs during the production room episode. There is
a brief shot, as Guido enters the production room, in which
the camera moves through the opening door as if it were
mounted on his shoulders. As a result of these and other
subjective shots scattered throughout 8-1/2, first-person

camera work becomes a basic motif which pervades the entire film.

In terms of the sound track, there is a technique which parallels Fellini's use of the subjective camera. Occasionally, on the sound track we can hear Guido's interior voice as he meditates upon his various problems. For instance, the transition between the first scene in the garden of the spa and the scene at the railroad station in which Guido meets Carla is bridged by the voice-over of Guido reading to himself Daumier's critical notes about his film script. Similarly, when Guido enters his room after his disheartening argument with Conocchia, we hear the sound of his interior voice expressing his deep-seated fears of being washed up as a creative artist. Later, after he has been called to Carla's room because she is ill, he lies upon her bed as we hear his interior voice preoccupied by the upcoming meeting with the Cardinal. Oblivious to Carla's agony, Guido thinks to himself, "What am I going to say to the Cardinal tomorrow?" Again, at the end of the film, we hear Guido's thoughts as he sits inside his automobile and begins to understand that he must reconcile himself to all the people who have touched his life.

These instances when interior monologues arise in 8-1/2 represent uses of the first-person narrative format which are more traditional, perhaps, than are the occasional instances of subjective camera work. Here we are privy to the protagonist's thoughts as we often are in fiction. In reality, however, the overt interior monologue is not so far removed in character from the first-person camera shot, for both enable us, in either verbal or visual form, to enter the protagonist's mind and share his inner thoughts and visions.

In a much more subtle sense, however, we are inside Guido's head throughout the entire film. As was suggested earlier, we move inside Guido's head whenever we are privy to his dreams, fantasies, memories, and hallucinations, all of which make up a considerable part of the film. Certainly all of the scenes devoted to Guido's mental phenomena, including transitory visions as well as extended fantasies, are unequivocal examples of the first-person narrative style.

Occasionally, in 8-1/2, there are moments when Guido's mental operations are portrayed with a particularly masterful subtlety. One of these moments occurs during the scene in which Guido and Carla have lunch in the dining room of her hotel. As Guido and Carla talk in the washroom we hear, in the background, the sound of a woman's voice humming a few bars of music. Carla has been babbling about a comic book she recently read when Guido, without listening, begins to paw her. She exclaims, "Guido be good! What do you want?" It is at this point that we first hear the music in the background. Although the tune is difficult to distinguish, the first few bars strongly resemble the rhumba which is later associated with Saraghina in the flashback of Guido's youthful adventure.

Significantly, after Carla leaves the washroom, the singing stops. It resumes, however, during the course of the meal. Briefly, we hear the woman singing immediately after Carla wipes her breasts with her napkin. It continues over the shot of Guido, totally bored, dangling her purse over the back of the chair. The tune is heard only briefly and quickly fades. It is even more difficult to discern but this time seems to resemble the tune associated with Guido's memory of his youthful wine bath at the family farmhouse rather than the Saraghina rhumba.

There is no visual indication that the tune emanates from any source physically present in the dining room. We see no woman singing, and there is no indication of a phonograph or a juke box being present in the room. Furthermore, the songs which the mysterious lady seems to be humming are reminiscent of those which are later associated with Guido's past.

From the available evidence, therefore, it seems clear that the female voice exists only in Guido's mind. The few brief bars of music which drift through the background of the dining room scene constitute a subtle aural flashback linking Carla, in Guido's mind, with the various women in his past associated with the music he conjures up, specifically Saraghina and the nurses at the farmhouse. This musical link is thematically significant, for we shall see that Carla is

essentially a successor to Saraghina and the farmhouse women
in terms of the role she plays in Guido's life. The fact
that tunes associated in Guido's memory drift fleetingly
through his mind when he first has lunch with Carla serves to
underline the relationship between Carla and these women from
Guido's distant past. This short episode serves as an indication of how thoroughly Guido's thoughts and mental processes
pervade the fabric of the entire film when the style of the
film is not overtly that of the first-person narrative.

One example of the predominance of Guido's point of view
throughout the entire film is particularly revealing. Despite the fact that the film clearly takes place in the year
in which it was made, the people who inhabit the spa are
dressed in the style of the early 1930's. Deena Boyer
remarks upon this incongruity in her book, The 200 Days of
8-1/2:

> All right, let's recapitulate. Guido is taking a
> walk in a spa in 1962. The people around him are dressed
> in the style of 1930. It is a way or projecting into
> the present the childhood memories with which he is
> obsessed at this time.[2]

Thus, even in those scenes which are not overtly cast in the
first-person mode, Guido's consciousness transforms the world
in which he lives. Thus, it can truly be said that the
entire film is structured in the cinematic equivalent of the
first-person narrative, for the entire work is pervaded and
shaped by Guido's consciousness. The audience's point of

[2]Deena Boyer, The 200 Days of 8-1/2 (New York, 1964),
p. 59.

view is consistently identified with Guido's, so that the world of 8-1/2 is perceived in terms of Guido's personal vision of it.

The entire film is so closely identified with Guido's consciousness, in fact, that his mental state is reflected even in its camera work. In 8-1/2 the camera is far more mobile than it is in any of Fellini's other films. His older films, such as La Strada, seem almost static by comparison. There are few shots in 8-1/2 in which the camera is stationary. The entire film, even down to the most ephemeral cut, is characterized by perpetual camera movement. 8-1/2 abounds in traveling shots of almost every variety. The conventional lateral, forward, backward, up, and downward movements are supplemented by a variety of unusual camera movements ranging from circular pans to traveling shots of such complexity that they defy a neat description. Fellini seems to be unable to resist the temptation to move the frame of his picture. Even during close-ups, when the subject is not moving and the camera remains stationary, Fellini will often zoom the lens in on the character slightly to underline the importance of a particular line of dialogue.

The most obvious use of the mobile camera during the film occurs during the long, extended shots in which camera movement, often highly complex and intricate, serves as the vehicle for changing the camera's orientation with respect to space and location, rather than the more conventional technique of film editing.

For instance, when, at the beginning of the film, we move from Guido's bathroom to the garden of the spa, the establishing shot of the garden is a long circular pan from right to left. A pervasive ambiance of decay and boredom is evoked by the languid camera movement circling past the elderly and infirm. An old lady fans herself while another smiles emptily and waves at the camera. An old man hands a glass of mineral water to a lady in a high-backed concrete chair. An old lady at a table smiles while another blows a kiss towards the camera. The camera circles left past them and finally rests on an old orchestra conductor in the foreground. Ironically, his orchestra is playing Wagner's Valkyrie theme which serves as background music to the scene.

This long, stately, circular establishing shot, however, is merely a prelude to a series of shorter but far more intricate shots in terms of camera movement, which serve to underscore further the ambiance of the spa. In this opening sequence, Fellini moves the camera in practically every possible direction. Beginning with the extended circular pan, the movement of the camera within the shots, in conjunction with the insistent martial rhythms of the Valkyrie theme, is juxtaposed to the torpor and lethargy of the people who inhabit the spa. They are old and seem scarcely able to move at all. When the camera does occasionally catch a glimpse of one of these patients walking along, it quickly passes him

by. The camera movements are not swift. In fact, they are
rather slow and stately. But in comparison to them, the
patients seem to hardly move at all. Lee Bobker in his book,
Elements of Film, comments upon the ironic manner in which
the various internal rhythms, created in these shots by the
music, camera movements, and editing, are juxtaposed to the
listlessness of the elderly guests:

> Consider the 'health spa' sequence in the early
> part of Fellini's 8-1/2. This sequence was edited to a
> fast moving Rossini overture. The scenes themselves,
> however, contain slow and languid rhythms that transmit
> a sense of idle purposelessness--a mood that gives this
> sequence its brilliant satiric quality. Thus, even
> though the music moves swiftly, filled with mercurial
> configurations typical of Rossini, the scenes convey a
> feeling of torpor--figures float by, the camera pans
> lazily past the guests, hands reach slowly for mineral
> water, and the camera dollies at an almost artificially
> retarded pace. In all, it is the internal rhythm of
> each scene that carries the mood and pace of the se-
> quence. Despite the frenetic pace of the music, the
> entire sequence transmits a mood of somnolence and
> death.[3]

This mood of somnolence and death is a reflection of one
of the major themes of 8-1/2, namely Guido's obsessive fear
of old age and death. Furthermore, the fact that all the
guests at the spa, particularly the women, are dressed in the
style of the early 1930's is, as Boyer has pointed out, a
projection of Guido's obsession with the past into the present. Moreover, the fact that the spa seems to be populated by

[3]Lee Bobker, Elements of Film (New York, 1969), p. 141.
(Bobker, I think, confuses the Valkyrie theme which serves as
the background music for this opening sequence at the spa
with the Rossini theme which follows after the sequence
ends.)

prelates and nuns of all sorts reflects the pervasive influence of the Church in Guido's world. Thus, this series of
establishing shots at the spa, establishes not only the ambiance of the spa, but also the pervasive influence of Guido's
major obsessions.

The most important thing to bear in mind at this time,
however, is that the extensive use of traveling shots in this
sequence is not an isolated incident within the film. Later
in the film single shots of even greater length and complexity than the initial circular pan of the spa occur, and these
shots replace more conventional cutting techniques entirely
as a means of moving the film through space and between incidents. For instance, in the first scene in the hotel lobby,
the opening shot is a single extended camera movement in
which the camera follows Guido, from the moment he leaves the
elevator, as he crisscrosses the lobby conversing with a
variety of assistants, agents, and hangers-on. The elabo-
rately choreographed shot does not conclude until Guido
finally leaves the lobby to greet the French actress who is
to play the role of his mother. Later a similar extended
shot occurs when Guido is on his way to his audience with the
Cardinal in the steam bath underneath the spa. Here the shot
is subjective. The camera seems to be inside Guido's head as
he moves swiftly through the underground corridors and is
approached by his various associates who give him clothes and
ask for special favors from the Cardinal. In a lengthy

continuous shot the camera shifts direction several times as
Guido follows one assistant after another as they rush
toward him from various directions.

Earlier it was indicated that all of this camera movement in the film serves to reflect the state of Guido's mind.
This statement can be better understood if we look at the
nature of the world through which the camera moves. Of
course, the extensive use of the mobile camera in 8-1/2
accentuates our sense of space in the film, so that many of
the scenes seem to unfold in large, open, and frequently
empty, spaces. The grand scale of the garden at the spa, the
empty reaches of the beach, and the sweeping desolation of
the cemetery in Guido's dream are all magnified by the mobility of the camera. Even the grandiose dimensions of the hotel
lobby are accentuated by the constant panning and tracking of
the camera.

At the same time, however, the hotel lobby seems to be
as amorphous as it is grandiose. It is difficult to establish concrete spatial relationships between the lobby and its
various extensions. Furthermore, this difficulty is even
more pronounced when the film moves outside the confines of
the hotel. There are few reliable landmarks by which we can
orient ourselves in Guido's world, and therefore we have
little sense of spatial relationships within it. The geography of 8-1/2 is nebulous and indeterminate. The continual
shifting of our point of view, due to the mobility of the

camera, only serves to increase this indeterminate quality.

There are no establishing shots, for instance, of the exteriors of the most important buildings in 8-1/2. We have no idea what the outside of Guido's hotel looks like, for there is not one establishing shot of the building's exterior in the entire film. Furthermore, there is also no establishing shot of the exterior of Carla's hotel in the film. Similarly, we have no idea what the exterior of other important buildings, such as the railroad station or Guido's childhood home, look like.

Even when exteriors, such as the garden of the spa or its outdoor cafe, are shown, we are never sure of their relationship to each other. The geography of the spa and its surrounding town is indeterminate. Moreover, the interiors of buildings have an amorphous quality about them. The relationship of corridors and rooms in Guido's hotel, for instance, is never fully established. At one point in the film, in fact, Fellini seems to purposely confuse the audience momentarily as to whether Guido is in his own hotel or Carla's. After he dreams of meeting his dead parents in a graveyard, while asleep in Carla's bed, we cut to a shot of Guido walking down a hotel corridor. We have no firm indication, however, as to where this corridor is. It is not until after Guido descends in an elevator to an ornate lobby below that we first realize he is no longer in Carla's cheap hotel but rather in the luxurious hotel at the spa.

The predominance of the moving camera throughout the film serves to accentuate the nebulous character of Guido's environment. He seems to live in a kind of limbo, devoid of architecture or landmarks. Furthermore, it is an indeterminate world of continual change and movement. Everything is in a constant state of flux, so that relationships between objects and places are constantly shifting.

The world in which Guido lives is a direct reflection of his personal situation. Guido has descended into a kind of personal limbo. He is unable to come to grips with the reality of his condition in the world, and his mind is continually shifting from the present into the past and, beyond that, into an imaginary world of fantasy and illusion. Since his relationship with external reality is tenuous at best, the perspective of the film perpetually shifts through a world of indeterminate shape and substance. Furthermore Guido perceives the world as lacking any central authority or order, and this fundamental uncertainty about the nature of the world contributes, along with his general mental condition, to the indeterminate quality of his environment as it is depicted on the screen.

The visual content of 8-1/2 reflects so directly Guido's state of mind, that even his deepest fears and obsessions have a visual equivalent. So pervasive is the first-person perspective in this film, that even Guido's deep-seated fear of death subtly shapes its visual content. There is a

consistent exaggeration of perspective throughout the film.
Often the settings are constructed to lead the eye towards
infinity and seem to point unmistakably towards something unknown beyond the physical world. Parallel lines, disappearing in a vanishing point beyond human perception, are consistently emphasized throughout 8-1/2.

Perhaps the most telling example of this compositional
style occurs during Guido's dream of meeting his parents in a
desolate graveyard. On one side of the screen a high brick
wall, stripped of its facing, stretches in a seemingly endless line disappearing into the infinite vanishing point.
Parallel to the wall, on the opposite side of the screen, a
row of large tombs similarly stretches towards the horizon,
joining the wall at the infinite point where parallel lines
meet. This exaggeration of perspective, leading the eye
towards the infinite, cannot be accidental, particularly in
the context of the graveyard setting.

The association of the infinite row of tombs with death
is self-evident. Yet, the visual composition of the entire
scene seems to point to the finite limits of human existence.
Its structure serves to draw the eye towards a point beyond
human perception, the point where parallel lines converge.
Implicit within this structure is a suggestion of the finite
limitations of man's perception and knowledge. Beyond this,
the association of the parallel lines with rows of tombs
implicitly suggests the finite character of human life as

well.

One might object, at this point, that it is not very remarkable to discover that the visual structure of Guido's dreams reflects his deepest fears and obsessions, in this case his fear of and obsession with death. We can, however, point out numerous instances throughout the film in which this particular mode of visual composition is repeated outside of Guido's dreams. The exaggeration of perspective, emphasizing the vanishing point, is a consistent motif throughout the film. The walls of the automobile tunnel in Guido's first dream, the design of the train station in which he meets Carla, the underground tunnels of the steam baths, and the rows of buildings in the plaza in which Claudia learns there will be no film all conform to this motif. All of them emphasize linear perspective and the ultimate vanishing point.

In this respect, it is significant that the corridor outside Guido's hotel room has a mirror at the end which exaggerates its depth by increasing the linear perspective of the walls which seem impossibly long, converging towards the vanishing point. This effect is particularly noticeable in the shot that directly follows the graveyard dream. In the shot that follows, introducing us to the next scene, Guido is awake again and walking gaily down the corridor outside his hotel room, towards the camera. The perspective of the corridor is exaggerated by the mirror at the end, and this effect is magnified by the fact that the camera draws away from Guido as he walks towards it, thus adding further to our sense of the hallway's depth. The exaggerated perspective of the hallway is clearly an echo of the exaggerated perspective of the graveyard in the previous scene. Once again, Guido's surroundings bear the stamp of his personality and concerns.

Significantly, the next time the film is situated in this hotel corridor, the setting is once again associated with death and old age. The heated argument between Guido and Conocchia takes place in this hallway, and the exaggerated perspective created by the mirror at the end of the hall is very much in evidence.

In most of the other settings in which the vanishing point motif is prominent, the automobile tunnel in Guido's first nightmare, the tunnels at the steam bath, and the plaza where Guido becomes disillusioned with Claudia, there are reminders of death and old age. His first nightmare ends with the deadly fall to earth. In the steam bath he has an audience with the cadaverous Cardinal. In the plaza, Claudia teases him because he dresses like an old man.

It is clear that even the visual composition of 8-1/2 is an extension, in many respects, of Guido's interior world. Just as the camera movement in the film reflects his feelings of uncertainty and confusion, its visual composition, at least in those scenes which emphasize the vanishing point, is a projection of Guido's obsessive fear of death and old age.

Thus, Guido's environment reflects the internal condition of his mind in a manner which is highly reminiscent of the first-person narrative or the internal monologue in literature.

The fact that Guido's consciousness pervades every scene of 8-1/2 is also reflected in the structure of the film. More precisely, the narrative structure of the film is inextricably identified with and completely dependent upon the flow of consciousness within Guido's mind. The structure of Guido's thoughts determines the structure of 8-1/2.

In other words, the film moves from reality to various dreams, fantasies, and memories as Guido's mind moves from one of these mental states to another. This is reflected in the temporal structure of the film which transcends the confines of linear clock time and flows, along with Guido's mind, through a kind of Bergsonian durée. Past, present, and imagination exist at once in Guido's world and intermingle in his mind, and the film records the effortless flow of his consciousness back and forth between them. Ultimately, the film emerges as a kind of stream-of-consciousness narrative.

Dwight McDonald, commenting on the protean nature of the film's constantly shifting levels of consciousness, keenly observed that, "Free association is its structural principle."[4] This idea that free association is the structural

---

[4]Dwight McDonald, "8-1/2, Fellini's Obvious Masterpiece," On Movies (New York, 1969), p. 18.

principle of 8-1/2 illustrates how deeply the film is identified with Guido's mind. The principle upon which the transition between scenes in the film is based is derived from the
mechanics of Guido's thought processes. This use of the
principle of free association as a transitional device in
8-1/2 is evident when various elements in Guido's environment, from words he hears to people he sees, trigger associations in his mind which launch him into a variety of rever-
ies, daydreams, and memories perceived, in the context of the
film, as entirely new scenes. The association serves as the
transitional device linking the scene in which it is triggered, usually in Guido's external environment, with the
scene in which it is completed, usually in Guido's interior
world.

Robert Gessner comments upon just this point in his
book, The Moving Image:

> The scene structure in 8-1/2 is more designed
> than generally recognized. Two main streams surge
> through the film: the narrative line concerning the
> frustrations over the pending film production and a
> parallel line composed of flashback dreams and psychic
> fantasies, meant to explore childhood motivations or
> adult escapes. Each fantasy or flashback is triggered,
> directly or indirectly, by a character who makes Guido
> become introspective, and these total eleven scenes.[5]

For instance, to cite one of the more obvious examples,
the magic word, "ASA NISI MASA," plucked from Guido's mind by

[5]Robert Gessner, The Moving Image (New York, 1968),
p. 259.

Maurice and Maya, triggers his memory of being bathed in wine
as a boy and provides a transition to the following scene
which takes place, in Guido's memory, at the family farmhouse
where he spent his early childhood. The exact nature of the
association is clarified later in the farmhouse scene when,
after the children have been put to bed, a young girl in the
bed across the room from Guido's invokes the magic words so
that the eyes on a picture on the wall will move and indicate
the way to buried treasure. The memory of the words themselves is probably triggered by Gloria when she tosses cherries to Guido and Mezzabotta earlier in the night club scene.
In his boyhood memory, we see the girl who later chants the
magic words perched on a trap door above the wine bath toss-
ing cherries down to the boys below.

Another striking example of the use of free association
as a structural principle in 8-1/2 occurs at the end of the
audience which Guido has with the Cardinal in the garden of
the spa. While the Cardinal and his clerical companions have
become absorbed by the singing of the Diomedes bird, Guido,
bored with the senile prelate and his entourage, looks about
and spots a grotesquely fat lady trudging down a hill in the
background. This vision triggers his boyhood memory of the
enormous prostitute, Saraghina. Although the associations
are not always as obvious as these, every movement from reality to fantasy in the film is triggered by some sort of association in Guido's mind between an element in the world that

surrounds him and an event in his past or an aspect of his
fantasy life.·

Guido's daydreams often arise as a means of escaping and
compensating for present difficulties. This is as true for
the ephemeral hallucinations and the relatively brief daydreams which occur within various scenes as it is for complex
fantasies, such as the harem episode, which constitute entire
scenes of their own. In other words, associations often
arise in his mind which serve to compensate for various difficulties he experiences. For instance, after his argument
with Conocchia, in which he is made to feel old and incompetent, he enters his hotel room tormented by the thought that
he is over the hill as both a man and an artist. Upon entering his room, he discovers that Claudia, his muse, awaits
him. Throughout the scene her presence serves to reassure
him as to his artistic and physical prowess.

We also find that associations are made, not only between Guido's external world and his interior world, but also
between many of the extended fantasies themselves. For instance, the harem fantasy is set in the farmhouse of Guido's
boyhood, which we have seen earlier in Guido's memory of
being bathed in wine. In fact the bath motif recurs throughout many of Guido's mental experiences. Guido is bathed in
wine as a boy, and is later bathed in the same vat during the
harem fantasies. In both scenes he is swathed in towels following the bath. The Cardinal is also bathed and wrapped in

towels during the steam bath fantasy. In a similar vein,
Guido, as a grown man, wears his schoolboy uniform when
visiting his parents during the graveyard dream.

The fact that the film is structured according to the
flow of consciousness within Guido's mind has led many viewers to feel that it is difficult to follow and impossible to
understand. Fellini, however, has provided many clues to
guide the audience through the many transitions from reality
to fantasy throughout the film. Thus, it is not as difficult
to differentiate between the two states of consciousness portrayed in the film as it might appear to the superficial
observer.

II. SIGNPOSTS OF THE IMAGINATION

Lighting

Many of the shifts from reality to fantasy in the film,
for instance, are accompanied by dramatic, and often violent,
changes in lighting. Often Fellini will underscore the movement from reality to fantasy by cutting from a scene situated
in the real world in which the screen is extremely dark to a
scene situated in Guido's consciousness in which the lighting
is almost painfully bright. For example, the film cuts
directly from the darkness of Carla's bedroom to the sun-
washed landscape of the cemetery. The movement from reality
into fantasy is underscored by the movement from darkness
into light.

Fellini takes some pains to make the contrast between the lighting of the two scenes as dramatic as possible. Guido, in the bedroom scene, asks Carla to draw the drapes, so that the bedroom is darkened as much as is possible. In the cemetery scene which follows, the film stock is greatly overexposed, so that the brilliance of the lighting seems to wash out many of the background details. Furthermore, the dream-like aspects of the scene are enhanced by the fact that the surrealistic glare which floods the cemetery defies the laws of nature. At first glance, the glaring light seems to wash out all shadows. The tall walls lining one side of the cemetery cast no shadow. Guido, his mother, and his father cast only tiny shadows, if indeed they cast any at all. The large tombstones which line the cemetery, however, cast shadows which are long and threatening.

This use of a violent contrast in lighting to mark the transition from reality to dream or fantasy recurs often throughout 8-1/2. At the beginning of the film, after Guido wakens from his nightmare, he walks from his dim bedroom into the bathroom. He turns on the flourescent bathroom lights, and as they flicker on they bathe the bathroom in a dazzling white light. The film then cuts to the garden of the spa which is awash with the glare of the Roman sun. While the scene at the garden does not take place in Guido's mind, the first brief vision of Claudia, Guido's muse, does take place while he waits for his glass of water. Thus, the transition

from darkness into light does coincide, at least, with a
transition from a scene which takes place in Guido's external
world, his bedroom, to one which, while still situated in his
external world, is characterized by the projection of a figure from Guido's imagination upon a realistic setting.

Similarly, following the scene in which Guido and Luisa
argue violently in their darkened bedroom, we cut to a
brightly lit open-air cafe. While this setting exists in
Guido's external environment, it is here that Guido, in order
to compensate psychologically for his wife's violent reaction
at spotting his mistress, fantasizes an amicable reunion between them. This brief daydream, in which Luisa and Carla
dance arm in arm, is a prelude to the grand harem fantasy
which follows.

These extreme contrasts between darkness and light in
the film are heightened by Fellini's use of a high contrast
film stock which produces dazzling whites and deep, inky
blacks while eliminating most shades of gray. Thus, when
Fellini cuts directly from a scene which is dimly lit to one
which is harshly overexposed, the effect is often quite
startling.

This pattern, however, of associating movement from
reality to fantasy with movement from darkness into light, is
fairly consistent throughout the film, even when the lighting
contrasts are not extreme. Fro instance, when the film cuts
from the night club at which Guido's mind is read to the

farmhouse of his childhood memory, the pitch black backgrounds of the open-air night club give way to the muted glow
of the farmhouse interior. While the change in lighting is
not startling, the movement from Guido's external environment
to his internal world is still accompanied by a general
brightening of the screen.

This is a pattern which is consistent throughout the
entire film. Only once is an imaginary episode accompanied
by the darkening of the screen. This occurs when Guido,
after his argument with Conocchia in the dimly lit hotel corridor, enters his darkened room and experiences a vision of
Claudia dressed as a chambermaid. The only other comparable
situation occurs when Guido catches a glimpse of the muse in
the darkened piazza when he is with Claudia, the actress.
Here, however, Guido imagines Claudia to be standing in a
brightly lit room painted white as he sees her through a
window.

Occasionally the light values will not change considerably in the transition from reality to fantasy. There is
little change when the film moves from the garden of the spa,
during Guido's audience with the senile Cardinal, to the
schoolyard where his friends entice him to visit Saraghina.
Both scenes are rather brightly lit.

Generally, however, the movement in and out of Guido's
head in the film is accompaned by rather marked changes in
lighting. This is not to say, however, that once the

lighting is intensified in scenes shaped by Guido's imagination it is consistently maintained at the same high level
throughout the scene. During the steam bath episode, for instance, the lighting darkens considerably as Guido rushes
from the white steam room to the dark sub-basement where he
has his audience with the Cardinal.

Similarly, when the fantasy of reconciliation between
Luisa and Carla at the cafe gives way to the more all-encompassing harem fantasy, the screen darkens noticeably. The
harem is more dimly lit than the outdoor cafe. Furthermore,
as the harem scene progresses, the screen continues to
darken, as the evening of Guido's self-indulgence passes into
night. During the revolt of the women, a single lamp, swing-
ing crazily from the rafters, illuminates the entire setting.
After the revolt is quelled, it is clear that we have passed
into night. Jacqueline's final dance is spotlighted against
a darkened room, and Guido makes his speech at a dinner table
lit only by small oil lamps. Interestingly, the memory of
the wine bath at the farmhouse takes place at the same time
of day so that the lighting also reflects the transition from
evening to night.

When one takes an overview of the entire film, he can
see that a general rhythmic pattern evolves from this use of
lighting to underscore the movement of the film narrative in
and out of Guido's mind. With only one real exception,
forced upon Fellini by circumstance and not representative of

his general design, the film develops a basic, cyclical pattern of gradually darkening the screen, usually as day passes into night, and then, as the picture is almost completely darkened, cutting suddenly to a scene which the screen is much brighter. Often the latter scene will be bathed in brilliant whites almost glaring in their intensity, contrasting violently with the darkness of the preceding scene.

Thus, the vivid contrasts in the film's lighting indicate not only the movement from fantasy to reality in 8-1/2 but also the cyclical passage of time in the film. Moreover, the rise and fall of Guido's fortunes, as the various days progress, are reflected in the changes in lighting as well. Both of these patterns, as well as the general interrelationships between fantasy and reality, are evident when one examines the comprehensive overview of the film provided by the synopsis in Appendix A.

The variations in the film's lighting also coincide with the natural rhythms of the day. 8-1/2 seems to take place over the period of a few days, and the chronology of these few days can be traced by following the pattern of the lighting in the film.

At the outset, it must be remarked that the fairly consistent adherence to chronology in this film is not necessarily typical of films as a whole. Few filmmakers trace the progress of their narratives on a day-to-day basis. Often there are huge gaps in the chronology of films. In 8-1/2, however, there is a consistent pattern of bright mornings and afternoons fading gradually into dusk, followed by the darkness of night. When this second lighting pattern is juxtaposed to the first, which was attuned to the passage of thoughts in Guido's interior world, fascinating patterns emerge. The chart on page 36 illustrates how the lighting patterns of the film, aside from the fantasy sequences, reinforce its tight chronology.

There is only one major discontinuity in the film, namely the leap from the night of the fourth day to the late afternoon of the fifth and last day. Despite this jump in chronology, Fellini continues to underscore the inexorable passage of time through the use of lighting, for the last scene begins in the dull light of late afternoon and concludes in the darkness of evening.

This pattern, of the gradual movement from day into night as it is reflected by changes in the film's lighting, is clearly imposed quite deliberately upon the film by Fellini, and its imposition imbues the entire work with a characteristic natural rhythm. The days of the film flow smoothly from dawn to dusk, and this flow is indicated by gradual changes in the lighting of the realistic scenes, as well as in the extended fantasies at the end of the film. Only the second day represents, in its sudden transition from day to night, a departure from this pattern, and there is abundant evidence which suggests that the character of the

THE CHRONOLOGY OF 8-1/2*

Day One	Day Two	Day Three	Day Four	Day Five
Sc. 1: Morning	Sc. 8: Morning	Sc. 12: 2 A.M. (the time on the hotel clock)	Sc. 24: Late morning--early afternoon	Sc. 28: Reality shifts to fantasy as the film moves from late afternoon through dusk to night.
Sc. 2: "	Sc. 9: "	Sc. 13: Early morning	Sc. 25: Fantasy experienced late morning--early afternoon. In fantasy day moves into night.	
Sc. 3: "	Sc. 10: Night	Sc. 14: "		
Sc. 4: Early afternoon	Sc. 11: Fantasy experienced at night.	Sc. 15: 4 A.M. (Guido tells Carla it is 4 A.M.)	Sc. 26: Night	
Sc. 5: "		Sc. 16: Late morning	Sc. 27: Fantasy experienced at night.	
Sc. 6: Late afternoon--dusk		Sc. 17: Fantasy experienced during the morning.		
Sc. 7: Fantasy experienced later, either dusk or nighttime.		Sc. 18: Afternoon		
		Sc. 19: "		
		Sc. 20: Dusk		
		Sc. 21: Night		
		Sc. 22: "		
		Sc. 23: Late night--early morning		

*The scene numbers above refer to the scenes this author out-lines in Appendix A.

second day, with its curious daytime scene in the hotel lobby, was a departure from Fellini's original plan to have the scene in the lobby occur during the evening of the first day.[6]

The lighting of 8-1/2 underscores the fact that the film embodies two different, if not contradictory, systems of time. On the one hand, Guido's thoughts flow through a kind of Bergsonian durée which transcends the inexorable march of linear clock time, and it is the lighting of the film which most directly underscores the transition from one temporal mode to another. On the other hand, Guido also is condemned to live, in a physical sense at least, within the confines of linear clock time, and this too is emphasized by the unmistakable use of lighting to indicate the steady passage from day to night within the film.

This, in a sense, is what the film is all about. Guido is a man obsessed by the inexorable passage of time, and particularly his life, towards old age and death. It is at the root of his deepest fears. Although Guido often attempts to

---

[6]There is considerable evidence to suggest that originally 8-1/2 was intended to span only four days. Apparently scenes eight and nine were to take place at night, thus making them an extension of the first day. Since the next two scenes take place at night, the first day would extend to scene eleven and the second day would be eliminated. The L'Avant-Scène script describes scenes eight and nine as taking place at night. See Federico Fellini, "Huit et Demi," L'Avant-Scène du Cinéma, No. 63, p. 20. Moreover, Deena Boyer describing scene nine in The 200 Days of 8-1/2 says, "According to the scenario, this was to be a night sequence. But here it is midmorning with a blindingly bright light" (Boyer, p. 166).

escape the myriad difficulties of his life by retreating into
his private fantasy world, he cannot escape the reality of
time. His mind can transcend the confines of linear clock
time, but his body remains in its grip.

It is this inexorable and pervasive quality of linear
time which is subtly underlined by the rhythmic repetition of
the daily waxing and waning of the light throughout the film.
Significantly, as the film progresses, the daily cycle of
light and darkness begins to pervade even Guido's fantasies,
as we have already seen. At first, in the early parts of the
film, his dreams and fantasies, such as the graveyard dream,
often run counter to time in the natural world. They are not
bound by the natural cycle of time. Yet, in the latter
stages of the film, even Guido's fantasies, in terms of their
lighting, conform to the chronology of the real world.
Chronological time, in the film, is all-pervasive and
inescapable.

The rise and fall of Guido's fortunes in 8-1/2, and
hence the progress of the dramatic narrative, also corre-
spond to the rhythmic variations in lighting throughout the
film, and more generally to the movement from day to night.
As a general rule, particularly in the latter stages of the
film, Guido's fortunes are at their lowest ebb during the
night, after darkness falls. Each day as the screen darkens,
Guido's difficulties begin to overtake him, until, on the
fourth night, when his producer announces the cocktail party,

they overwhelm him. The brutal argument with Conocchia, the
bedroom quarrel with Luisa, the breakup of his marriage, and
the final admission to Claudia that there is no film all take
place at night.

Conversely, in the mornings of the film there is often a
feeling, however transitory, of rebirth and renewal.
Fellini's wry depiction of the spa filled with light and
orchestral music, however incongruous the context, seems a
welcome relief from Guido's nightmares and his gloomy bedroom
filled with doctors and nurses. Similarly, the garden of the
spa, filled with light, is a welcome diversion from the
fevered atmosphere of Carla's bedroom.

At the end of the film, however, the pattern is reversed.
The movement from darkness to light at the beginning of the
hallucinatory press conference offers Guido no respite. By
then, however, fantasy is no longer a vehicle for escape.
The forces which oppress him invade even his dream world. At
the film's end it is the coming of evening which brings him
the soothing fantasy of the grand reconciliation between all
the people in his life. Thus at the end of 8-1/2 the movement from light to darkness is now a movement from despair to
reconciliation.

The contrast between light and darkness is so fundamental to the basic structure of 8-1/2 that it extends even to
the costuming. Throughout the film, in conjunction with the
lighting patterns, the color white is often associated with

those things which Guido values most highly in his fantasy life. These qualities which characterize Guido's most pleasurable fantasies, reconciliation, submission, and purity, are epitomized by his dream lady, Claudia, and she always appears in his visions wearing white. In fact, when the real Claudia appears at the end of the film, we know that Guido is in trouble because she is wearing black.

Furthermore, throughout the film, as we have seen, whiteness is conspicuously associated with his fantasies, suggesting therefore that they are imbued with these values. The blazing sun which pervades the cemetery dream or Saraghina's beach, for instance, is a kind of whiteness. The whiteness of the open air cafe, both as a result of the intensity of the sun and the color of its decor, indicates that the unpleasantness of Luisa's confrontation with Carla is merely a prelude to the farmhouse fantasy.

The real culmination of the whiteness motif, as it relates specifically to costuming, however, occurs during the last scene in the film. One of the major visual motifs of the final scene is the whiteness which characterizes the costuming of all the major figures in Guido's reconciliation fantasy. Never in the entire film is whiteness so strikingly associated with both Guido's fantasies and the need for love and reconciliation which they embody. All of the major figures in Guido's life, his parents, the prelates, Carla, Saraghina, Rosella, and Luisa are dressed, like Claudia, in

white. They all become identified with the qualities
embodied in Guido's earlier fantasies. Only Guido, at the
end of the film, among all the major characters, still wears
black, but the school uniform of his boyhood incarnation has
been transformed from black to white.

Sound

Fellini also uses music to distinguish fantasy from
reality in the film. The musical backgrounds in the film's
realistic scenes, with one possible exception, all emanate
from sources which are explicitly shown upon the screen. The
music which we hear is always justified in terms of verisimilitude. All the music stems from Guido's natural environment, and when there is no possible source for music in a
scene, we hear none on the screen. This concern for verisimilitude in terms of musical backgrounds in the film, however, does not extend to fantasy sequences, and the music in
these scenes almost always emanates from unseen sources.

In the first scene at the garden of the spa, for instance, the themes from Wagner and Rossini which constitute
its musical background are clearly shown to emanate from an
orchestra playing in the bandshell in the garden. Similarly,
at the night club in Scene 10 the background music to which
the various couples are dancing is provided by a band. The
first shot of the scene which takes place in the steam baths
of the spa shows a small band playing the music heard on the

sound track. When Guido meets his wife at the arcade in town, we hear the sound of "Blue Moon" in the background. The scene is introduced by a shot of an open-air cafe across from the arcade where a band is playing in the distance.

The only substantial exception to this pattern occurs after Guido meets Claudia, the actress, in the movie theater. As they leave the theater, an orchestra begins to play with increasing volume. It is a dance number reminiscent of the music of the thirties, which is consistent with the thirties motif of the film. In a way, it is reminiscent of the reunion between Guido and Luisa, which had the music of "Blue Moon" as a background. There is no visible source for this background music. Although the outdoor cafe, which has had a band in other scenes, seems to be across the street from the theater, the visual connection is not really made. Nowhere in the sequence is an orchestra of any kind visible. The scene is merely an exception to the general rule of the film, a single deviation from the norm.

On the other hand, Guido's fantasies and memories are usually characterized by musical backgrounds without a visible source. In the fantasies the background music is never bound by any sense of verisimilitude. Furthermore, within the fantasies two major musical themes are developed.

The first is the nostalgic musical theme associated with Guido's boyhood at the farmhouse. During Guido's memory of being bathed in wine lees, we hear this theme sung by a woman

in a manner reminiscent of the singing heard during Guido's
lunch with Carla. Despite the fact that this plaintive tune
is heard throughout the early part of the farmhouse episode,
no naturalistic source for it is portrayed upon the screen.
The music merely exists in Guido's mind, in association with
this memory.

A second major musical motif associated with Guido's
memories arises during the Saraghina episode. The tune of
the rhumba she dances on the beach becomes a leitmotif which
recurs at various times throughout the film. In terms of the
episode itself, however, the tune exists only in Guido's
mind. As Saraghina dances the rhumba in Guido's memory we
hear it being played by a band which exists only on the sound
track of the film or in Guido's memory as he visualizes the
episode.

The harem fantasy follows an identical pattern. Many
musical themes found throughout the film, such as Saraghina's
rhumba and the Valkyrie theme, are interwoven in this fantasy, but an orchestra is never depicted playing them on
screen. The source remains within Guido's mind. As we share
his memories and fantasies, he colors them with musical associations which spring from his consciousness alone.

Only the final two fantasies in 8-1/2 deviate from this
pattern, and only the last one represents a truly significant
deviation. During the nightmarish press conference, a band
is shown on screen, early in the episode, which does seem to

be playing the frantic music which pervades the scene. In realistic terms, however, the band is much too small to be responsible for the orchestral background music. The band has only a few pieces while the background music is played by a symphony orchestra with a full violin section. Therefore, even in this fantasy there is no real relationship between the background music and its supposed source.

Only in the final, climactic fantasy of the film is an orchestra shown which is capable of playing the music we hear on the sound track. In this scene we do see a full piece orchestra seated on a podium next to the launching tower. Like the scene in which Guido meets Claudia, this scene must be viewed as a deviation from the general pattern established in the film with respect to the sound track.

In terms of the sound track, another association made with Guido's fantasies, or with scenes in which fantasies occur, is the sound of the wind. In the opening fantasy, as Guido soars through the clouds, we hear the sound of the wind blowing furiously through the heavens. It is a sound which recurs again and again throughout the film, almost always in conjunction with Guido's fantasy life.

During the montage, for instance, which concludes the ASA NISI MASA episode, we hear the wind blowing through the empty courtyard of the farmhouse as the camera cuts through its deserted corridors. Later, the use of the wind in con-junction with Guido's fantasies is particularly striking near

the end of the film. When Guido takes Claudia to the deserted piazza, we hear the wind blowing through the courtyard. While the scene is realistic, the fantasy of seeing
Claudia, the muse, in the piazza does occur here. In the
press conference fantasy which follows, we can hear the wind
howling even more strongly across the beach, and it seems
that, in Guido's mind, the wind from the piazza at night is
transferred to the fantasy which follows. Throughout the
rest of the film, the wind remains a constant motif. After
the press conference fantasy concludes with Guido's suicide,
the wind continues to blow through the launching tower site
as Guido, now in reality, orders it torn down. Then at the
end of the film, as he slips back into fantasy, the wind continues to blow in the background of his final dream of reconciliation. At the end of the picture, after Guido's incarnation as a child marches off screen, it is the final sound we
hear.

Gestures

Another device which both distinguishes Guido's fantasies from reality and provides a link between them is the
repetition of certain key gestures by various people. For
instance, in the nightmare which opens the film, just before
the mysterious fumes begin pouring into Guido's car, he picks
up a cloth lying on top of the dashboard and wipes the window
of the car with a distinctive circular motion. The same

motion is repeated by Guido's mother when she enters Carla's bedroom at the beginning of the cemetery dream and wipes the wall with a cloth. In the next shot the wall is transformed to glass, a window of a crypt in the graveyard. Thus, it seems that the magical power of transmutation resides within the gesture. This gesture occurs again, when during the Saraghina episode the prostitute massages the stucco wall of the abandoned sea front structure with the same circular motion. As a motif appearing only in Guido's fantasies, this gesture is one means of distinguishing fantasy from reality.

Another gesture which becomes a kind of leitmotif linking certain of Guido's fantasies is the flying gesture. In at least two key moments of the film, a gesture is made by crossing the arms in front of the chest and flapping the hands, as if in imitation of a bird's wings. The gesture first occurs during Guido's farmhouse memory. When the young girl in the bed across from Guido's invokes the magic words, "ASA NISI MASA," she also makes this flying gesture. Later, during the harem scene, which is situated in the same farmhouse, Guido makes the identical flying motion while floating contentedly in his bath. This flying motion is just one of an entire series of images related to flying which arise in the film, and which will be discussed in far greater detail later in the paper.

There is also one striking gesture which becomes a recurrent motif in Guido's real world and which is consistently

used to indicate that the film is about to move into the
realm of fantasy. This is Guido's habit of rubbing his nose
or pulling his glasses down his nose as he begins to launch
into one of his fantasies. The gesture of pulling his
glasses down his nose indicates that Guido is beginning to
look inward rather than outward at the world around him. The
tapping or rubbing of the nose often serves as a prelude to a
fantasy. When Guido pulls his glasses down at the same time,
a fantasy or memory almost always follows.

Often the gesture is associated with fantasies about
women. Guido pulls his glasses down his nose when he envisions Claudia at the spa. He repeats the gesture when his
glimpse of an enormous lady trudging down a hill triggers his
memory of Saraghina. Guido's fantasies, however, are not
exclusively about women. His fantasy of the steam bath audience with the Cardinal is introduced in a fashion similar to
those above. The fantasy begins when Guido's glasses cloud
over as he sits in the steam bath indicating, like the gesture
of pulling down his glasses, that he is now looking within
his mind.

Internalized Motifs

Up to this point we have discussed only motifs which
recur in fantasy sequences or in conjunction with them.
Sometimes, however, images which Guido perceives in his external environment reappear in his thoughts in new and

different contexts. They have been internalized by his subconscious.

For instance, when Guido asks Carla to make a face like
a whore during their bedroom scene, she leers at the camera
in a caricature of carnal lust. The expression recurs in
Guido's memories and fantasies. Saraghina, during her
rhumba, makes the same expression. Later, during the harem
fantasy, when Guido grants to the black girl who also dances
to the tune of Saraghina's rhumba, but with far more grace
and skill, permission to remain in the harem, she turns to
the camera and smiles like a whore.

The cape motif works in a similar fashion. Guido as a
schoolboy always wears a cape. This motif extends from
Guido's memories into his everyday life and then into his
dreams and fantasies. In the opening nightmare, Guido's coat
flaps behind him like a long black cape as he soars into the
sky. Later in the hotel lobby, Cesarino spreads Guido's coat
in front of the camera like a cape. The persistence of this
motif in Guido's adult life serves to indicate that Guido, in
many respects, is still a boy. This becomes explicit during
the cemetery dream when Guido, the adult, is garbed in the
uniform of his schoolboy days. Not only does this suggest
that Guido's parents still see him as a little boy, but it
also hints at the arrested development of certain aspects of
his personality.

People are wrapped in towels throughout the film. Guido

remembers being wrapped in towels after his boyhood bath in wine lees. At another point Carla apears in her bedroom wrapped in a towel while wearing a small black hat. In the harem fantasy Guido is once again wrapped in towels, and this time he too wears a black hat. All the men in the steam bath are wrapped in towels. The Cardinal is wrapped in a towel during the steam bath audience. Thus, once again, the motif appears in all three levels of Guido's existence: memory, reality, and fantasy.

The free association process which triggers Guido's memories and fantasies falls into this pattern. The fat lady Guido sees on a hill reminds him of Saraghina and triggers his memory of her. When Gloria tosses grapes to Guido and Mezzabotta at the night club, he is reminded of the girl who tossed grapes to the boys in the farmhouse memory. Since she is also the girl who chants the words "ASA NISI MASA," they are on Guido's mind when his thoughts are read by Maurice and Maya, at which point the film shifts from the night club to the farmhouse.

All of this, of course, indicates the extent to which the film is structured upon the flow of Guido's consciousness. Guido's consciousness is not confined to linear clock time but, rather, exists in a kind of Bergsonian durée. One gets much the same sense of time in this film as Suzanne Budgen describes in Juliet of the Spirits, a film which, if anything, presents the stream of consciousness with even greater complexity:

> There is throughout the film a repetition of
> shapes, and occasionally of sounds, providing a
> link between certain sequences which is independent
> of time, and in some degree flattening out, so to
> speak, the time element which is imposed by the
> necessary sequence of frames. This gives the film
> a descriptive, rather than a narrative, quality, as,
> with parts of one sequence being called to mind in
> the middle of another, there is a sense in which
> the whole film is present all the time.[7]

This sense that the whole film is present all the time is
strong in 8-1/2 and certainly represents a distinctive feature of Fellini's style at this time.

III. GUIDO: A PORTRAIT

The Male Menopause

The memories he recalls, the fantasies he creates, and
even the things he looks at when the point of view of the
camera becomes identical to his, all tell us a great deal
about Guido. All the aspects of his mental life coalesce, so
to speak, into a psychological biography of the man. We become acquainted with his most deep-seated fears and motiva-
tions, as well as the forces which have shaped them throughout his life. One even gets a sense of Guido's personal
development, even though the film is in no sense a

---

[7]Budgen, p. 71. Juliet is both more complex and more
subtle. Even shapes in Juliet's world reappear in new contexts in her fantasies and memories. For instance, the black
shrouds which cover the erotic statues in the sculptress's
studio ironically remind her of the nuns at her childhood
convent school, so that they too wear these shrouds when we
see them in her memory.

chronological biography of his life. Rather, this sense of
his personal development arises from seeing which incidents
from his past occupy his memory and which elements from his
subconscious seep into his fantasies.

It has been said, for instance, that the film traces the
growth of Guido's sexuality. Rather than presenting a chronological sexual biography, however, the film traces this
growth by intoducing us, through his memories, dreams, and
fantasies, to all the women he has ever known, loved, or even
merely desired, and by showing us the kind of influence these
various women have had upon his life. In the process, of
course, we also learn much about his attitudes towards women.

Before we can discuss the specific content of Guido's
fantasies, however, we must first examine the factors which
motivate them. Guido, as we find him in the beginning of the
film, is fundamentally an artist who has dried up creatively.
Guido's artistic blockage, however, is merely one aspect of a
more all-encompassing spiritual and emotional paralysis. Not
only is Guido unable to make his film, he is also unable to
make any decisions about the course of his life and his marriage. A number of factors contribute to this paralysis,
including Guido's rejection of the moral authority of the
Church, his inability to love, his fear of old age and death,
and his lack of self-knowledge.

In contemporary terms, we would say that Guido's behavior in the film reflects the classic symptoms of the male

menopause. He is obsessed with old age and death, and in order to evade these grim realities he sinks more and more into a web of memories and fantasies in which he dotes upon his past. Guido, in this film, always looks behind him; he never looks ahead.

The manifestation of this obsessive fear in the film is not limited to Guido's behavior. Fellini creates, in the film, a pervasive ambiance of old age and death, and Guido merely acts within this context of this environment.

Guido's external environment is permeated by images of death. Dwight McDonald suggests that aging is a major theme in the film. He points to the elderly patients at the spa, the senile Cardinal, Mezzabotta who doggedly attempts to dance with Gloria, the French actress who attempts to seduce Guido, and the dowager who hopes to live another hundred years as characters and incidents reflecting the theme of aging. This theme, however, is also reflected in countless images of old age which are an inherent part of the fabric of Guido's everyday reality.

The basic ambiance of the spa, which is the main setting for the film, is that of old age and physical decay. A spa, after all, is a place patronized by elderly people who seek some cure, or at least relief, from the infirmities of old age. The major vehicle for this cure is water, and, in this context, water becomes a primary motif in the film which will be examined extensively at a later point in this paper. For

ur purposes now, however, the most significant aspect of the
pa is that it is inhabited by hordes of elderly people,
hose presence becomes representative of Guido's own obsession
ith old age.

For instance, the extended establishing shot which intro-
uces the audience to the garden of the spa is essentially a
anorama of physical decay and old age. The single most im-
ortant fact about the spa is that it is inhabited by people
waiting death with vacant smiles and glasses of mineral
ater. The shots which follow extend this motif; they con-
titute a montage of physical debilitation epitomized by the
lose-up of a palsied hand clutching a cane.

This ambiance of death and decay extends throughout all
he scenes situated at the spa. The nightclub, for instance,
s populated almost exclusively by elderly people dancing
tiffly to the band as if in rigor mortis. As the pace of
he music quickens, Mezzabotta sweats profusely as he strug-
les to keep up with the spirited dancing of his young
iance. Later an old lady's mind is read by Maurice and Maya.
ccording to Maya, "She would like to live another hundred
ears."

After this scene, we return to the lobby of the hotel at
ight. Here, the aging French actress, whom Guido has hired
o play his mother, makes a pathetic attempt to seduce him.
hen Guido does not respond to her advances she begins to
reak down emotionally. "I'm a very sensual woman," she

pleads, "and a naughty one too." Her desperation is that of a woman, once young and attractive, who has lost her power t interest men. Her obvious sense of loss is directed, not to wards Guido, but, rather, towards her lost youth.

The theme of old age and death pervades the rest of the film as well. Guido receives a call from Carla who is sick with fever in her hotel room. When he arrives, it becomes rather clear that she is suffering from the hot flashes asso ciated with the onset of menopause. The next day, Guido has his audience with the Cardinal, who is hopelessly old and senile. Later, he descends with his producer, into the stea room beneath the spa's hotel, which is inhabited by old men wrapped in towels. We see them slumped, almost lifeless, on the benches which surround the room.

Beyond the fact that Guido's world is pervaded by the elderly, people are always confronting him with the reality that time is running out on him. The most explicit presenta tion of this theme, perhaps, occurs when the producer gives Guido the gift of a watch. Throughout the film, temporal demands are made upon Guido. Constantly, he is harrassed by various associates, agents and newsmen who want to know when he will be ready to make his film. Always, he is being con fronted with the fact that, in the eyes of all these people, time has run out for him. Even when Guido turns to Rosella' spirits for solace and advice the answer is the same. Rosella tells him that, "They say that you're free. But you

ave to choose and you don't have much time left. You have
o choose soon."

There is also a striking emphasis upon the ages of
people within the film. The numbers by which people gauge
their mortality intrude upon many scenes, and form a kind of
leitmotif in which their ages are either specified or revealed. People constantly lie about their age throughout the
film, as if that could somehow make them younger, and occasionally these lies are exposed to ridicule as pitiful
paxes.

The film has scarcely begun before the doctor examining
Guido after his nightmare asks him his age. Guido answers
that he is forty-three. Later, during his audience with the
Cardinal in the garden, the Cardinal asks Guido the same
question. Once again Guido answers that he is forty-three.
Thus, Guido is situated precisely in terms of his chronological age.

The motif of citing ages appears in other scenes as
well. At the beginning of the night club scene, an old lady
whispers cattily to another, "I saw her passport. She's
fifty-two." In a similar vein, Jacqueline Bonbon, the aging
dancer, ludicrously maintains that she is only twenty-six
when she is ordered to go upstairs to join the women who have
become too old to please Guido. When Guido auditions old men
for the part of his father in his film, he asks each man how
old he is. Once again the mortal numbers echo through the

sound track as they answer in turn, "seventy, . . . sixty-four, . . . sixty-eight."

When Guido asks these men their ages, his deep-seated fear of old age is unmasked for the first time. After the second one answers, the film cuts back to Guido. He is looking at them critically, and a note of bitterness, and yet at the same time sadness, has crept into his expression. After the third one answers his question, Guido seems to sadden even more. He tells Conocchia, "They're not old enough." Cesarino is incredulous and points to the most pathetic of the group. "What!" he exclaims, "This one's ready to drop dead!" Guido, however, abruptly turns his back on them. Guido's abrupt and rather cruel dismissal of the old men suggests that somehow their appearance touches a raw nerve. One senses a deep-seated anxiety underlying his actions.

There are other instances when Guido displays uneasiness and even anger in the presence of old people. During his conversation with Rosella at the launching pad, for instance, he cruelly toys with an old sailor who is working on the set. He asks the sailor to do the dance he learned in America and promises him a part in his film. The old sailor chants a sing-song tune and dances while Guido looks on apparently amused. When he resumes his conversation with Rosella, and the sailor interrupts to ask what part he will get, Guido cruelly shouts at him to "Go away!"

Guido's behavior here seems almost out of character. He

is seldom cruel towards others. But these episodes all have
one factor in common. In each instance, Guido's cruelty is
directed towards elderly people.

The underlying cause of this curious behavior becomes
clear during Guido's most brutal confrontation with an elderly person, his argument with Conocchia in the hotel corridor.
Conocchia, upset because Guido has ignored his offers of help
and advice, shouts "Look I've been in this business for
thirty years, and I've made pictures none of you would have
the guts to try." Guido shouts back furiously, "Stop shouting you old fool." Suddenly Conocchia's defiance is crushed.
Tears flood his eyes. "So you finally said it . . . old," he
answers. Then he leans against the wall and weeps. Suddenly
the central issue is exposed. It is the word "old" which
causes Conocchia to lose his composure. He finally understands the rather brutal fact that Guido has rejected his
help and his advice throughout the film precisely because he
is old. In the process we learn something very important
about Guido. It is clear that his rejection of Conocchia because he is an old man is a reflection of a deep-seated anxiety about old age itself.

In this context, it is significant that this scene takes
place in the hotel corridor, with its heavy emphasis upon
parallel lines stretching to the vanishing point. As mentioned earlier, parallel lines, as a visual motif, are associated with death in the graveyard episode, and all

subsequent scenes in which they appear must bear the weight
of this association.

The argument concludes with a warning which cuts to the
heart of Guido's deepest fears. Conocchia warns Guido, "You
need younger people around you, but watch out, you're not the
man you used to be." Thus, at the end, it is Guido who is
implicitly accused of being old and incompetent. As Guido
enters his dark bedroom he is riddled by self-doubt. As we
hear his interior voice on the sound track, he thinks, "A
lack of inspiration . . . that's it. And suppose it's not
temporary Guido old man? Suppose you're really finished you
uninspired, untalented fake." For the first time in the film
the hidden fear which underlies Guido's hostility to old
people is stated explicitly. He is terrified by the thought
that, as he begins to enter middle age, he is losing his
creative power. Guido is deeply conscious of the fact that
he is not the man he used to be, and it terrifies him. Guido
is hostile toward the elderly because they remind him of his
ultimate destiny.

Guido's actions are not the only aspect of his behavior
which reveals his obsession with old age. His fantasies,
memories, and dreams are filled with images of old age and
death. The first scene in the film, Guido's nightmare, ends
with the director falling from the sky to his death on the
beach below. Significantly, Guido's next dream occurs in a
cemetery. If the first dream depicts death as a terrifying

fall, the second paints it in far more reassuring terms. In the cemetery Guido meets his parents and discovers that, for them, death seems merely to be a continuation of life at its most prosaic level, in a slightly different context. Guido's father, for instance, complains about the accomodations. The entire scene is played as if Guido were visiting his parents at their new home in some distant city. Certainly this dream is as symptomatic of Guido's obsessive fear of death as the earlier nightmare was, only in a different sense. This dream is a kind of wish-fulfillment dream, in that it denies the finality of death. Death is depicted in the most mundane terms. This is a vision of death as Guido would like to believe in it. The very absurdity of the mundane existence which he visualizes his parents leading beyond the grave reveals the lengths to which his psyche will go to deny the finality of death.

Other images of old age and death intrude on Guido's fantasies. In his imaginary audience with the Cardinal in the steam bath, the Cardinal seems particularly old, emaciated, and senile. The threat of old age and death lurks in the background of the harem fantasy. In Jacqueline Bonbon, the aging cafe dancer, the ravages of old age are parodied. Yet, the upstairs room to which she is relegated, along with the other old and useless women, remains as an implicit threat to all the harem girls. Furthermore, even Guido's youth and virility are questioned. When the women revolt, the French

actress says, "What makes him think he's still young? He's a
lousy lover." She then accuses Guido of impotence, "Talk and
kisses, that's speed. Then he goes to sleep." The motif of
old age and death in Guido's fantasies culminates, of course,
during the hallucinatory press conference at the end of the
film. Unable to face the accusations of the reporters, Guido
crawls under the conference table and commits suicide.

In a visual context, there seems to be a definite association between the theme of time and aging and Fellini's
proclivity for shooting people in silhouette. The film is
studded with silhouettes of various characters, and occasionally the technique suggests that these people are literally
passing into the shadows.

This use of the silhouette occurs most poignantly at the
beginning of the graveyard dream. Momentarily, as Guido
enters the graveyard, he is literally transformed into a
shade. As it begins, we see Guido's face is silhouetted in
close-up on the left side of the screen as he watches his
mother. Silhouetted against the dazzling light which pervades the cemetery, he quite literally becomes a shadow in
the nether world of the dead. In a sense, he enters into
death itself.

Similarly, the Cardinal is silhouetted upon a towel held
in front of him as he prepares for his mud bath. His features are grotesquely distorted so that his nose appears unnaturally long. The association of the silhouette with death

arises from the cadaverous appearance of the Cardinal, as well as the hellish ambiance of the steam bath in which Guido fantasizes the scene. Even his walk to see the Cardinal has the air of a descent into the underworld.

At the end of the press conference, Guido commits suicide surrounded by wildly distorted silhouettes. After he slips underneath the conference table to commit suicide, on the tablecloth draped over the edge of the table, we see the grotesque shadows of the reporters looming up next to him. The threatening silhouettes of distorted heads and hands which seem to surround him are a visual representation of a mind out of control and of the suicidal impulses which arise from Guido's ensuing panic. Of course, they reflect these fears both in Guido, the man within the fantasy, and Guido the fantasizer.

This association of silhouettes with suicide indicates that there is a paradoxical dimension to Guido's obsessive fear of old age and death which deserves at least a brief mention. As much as Guido fears death he also seems, in a different sense, to desire it. Throughout the film he behaves in ways which can only be termed self-destructive. Clearly unable to make his film, he still insists upon gathering an ever growing retinue about him in the desperate hope that somehow, by some mystical process, the film would suddenly coalesce in his mind. In the end the desperate gamble proves his undoing. Driven by guilt feelings, he

invites his wife to the spa even though his mistress had already arrived. This action ultimately results in the collapse
of Guido's marriage. Thus, there is clearly a self-destructive strain in Guido's behavior which is most explicitly revealed in his dream of suicide at the end of the press conference fantasy. Certainly in the suicide there is a sense
in which Guido, at his most desperate moments, desires death
as an escape from the problems which overwhelm him. Moreover, in terms of his behavior, Guido clearly draws together
personally all the forces which ultimately crush him.

We must also temper our analysis of Guido's fear of old
age and death by pointing out that this fear is, to a certain
extent, counterbalanced by a profound boredom with life.
This boredom is represented, not so much in terms of visual
images, but rather in terms of Guido's behavior. His every
mannerism is weighted with a heavy sense of ennui.

At the night club of the spa, for instance, Guido's
weary expression belies his boredom with his friends' empty
chatter. To amuse himself, he molds a false nose made of
dough. Morevoer, he is bored with his wife and has a mistress. He is also bored by her, however, and when they eat
lunch he slouches in his chair dangling her purse, an all too
obvious Freudian symbol, while mocking her aimless chatter by
twittering in sing-song tones.

Guido is a man who is excited only by the unattainable.
In his mind he conjures up visions of an ideal woman, embodied

by Claudia his muse, totally unattainable in terms of flesh and blood. When the real Claudia arrives at the spa, she too quickly begins to bore Guido. As far as people in the real world go, only the mysterious lady at the spa, played by Caterina Boratto, whom Guido will never meet, interests him.

Thus Guido, terrified with death but bored with life, is trapped in the classic cycle of pain and ennui which the German philosopher Schopenhauer described as the natural condition of mankind.[8] Desire is a kind of pain, but with satisfaction, particularly when it is too easily obtained, comes boredom. Guido attracts women with ease, but is soon bored with them. The only women, therefore, who are equal to his desires, are the unattainable women of his fantasies.

The fact that Guido experiences two such deeply contradictory feelings simultaneously is partly responsible for the spiritual paralysis which stifles him in this film. Alternately bored and afraid, he is a man unable to make any choices in his life or his art. Unable to resolve this dilemma, Guido attempts to escape from a world of impotence and frustration into an imaginary world of memories, dreams, and fantasies.

There is an adolescent quality to these memories,

---

[8]"We saw that the inner being of unconscious nature is a constant striving without end and without rest. . . . Thus its life swings like a pendulum backwards and forwards between pain and ennui." Arthur Schopenhauer, The World as Will and Idea, trans. R. B. Haldane and J. Kemp (Garden City, 1961), p. 323.

dreams, and fantasies which is unmistakable. Guido's memories are exclusively those of childhood, and his fantasies
are distinctly adolescent in character. His fantasies are
almost always about women, and Guido inevitably views them
through adolescent eyes. In Guido's dreams, as opposed to
his life, his women are always completely subservient to his
every whim, and devote their every moment to his pleasure.
This role is epitomized by Claudia, his ideal woman. Guido
has the body of a forty-year-old man and the sexual outlook
of an adolescent.

This adolescent aspect of Guido's psychology has been
commented upon by other writers. William S. Pechter points
out that, "The theme of the director's fixation on his childhood permeates the film, embodied in such recurrent figures
as his mother, his dead father, and the grotesquely voluptu-
ous whore from whom he took his sexual education in defiance
of his authorized educators, the ubiquitous priests."[9] Ted
Perry suggests that Fellini considers Guido "imprisoned in
his boyhood": ". . . In an interview, Fellini has said 'that
society's norms and rules imprisoned Guido in his boyhood
with a sense of guilt and frustration. . . .'"[10]

This regression back to adolescence, and even youth, is

[9]William S. Pechter, Twenty-four Times a Second (New
York, 1960), p. 79.

[10]Ted Perry, "Signifiers in Fellini's 8-1/2," Forum
Italicum, 6 (March, 1972), 80.

a phenomenon which often accompanies a man's advancement into middle age. Like Guido, many men, unable to accept the fact that they are growing old, seek the comfort of youthful fantasies. Dr. Jung, in his book Modern Man in Search of a Soul, deals with this aspect of the male menopause in some detail:

> The very frequent neurotic disturbances of adult years have this in common, that they attempt to carry the psychic dispositions of youth beyond the threshold of the so-called years of discretion. . . . The neurotic is rather a person who can never have things as he would like them in the present, and who can therefore never enjoy the past.
> As formerly the neurotic could not escape from his childhood, so now he cannot part with his youth. He shrinks from the grey thoughts of approaching age; and, feeling the prospect before him unbearable, is always straining to look behind him. Just as a childish person shrinks back from the unknown in the world and in human existence, so the grown man shrinks back from the second half of life.[11]

Furthermore, Jung relates this sentimental longing for youth to a "craving for pleasure and power" which certainly characterizes many of Guido's daydreams:

> Something in us wishes to remain a child; to be unconscious, or, at most, conscious only of the ego; to reject everything foreign, or at least subject it to our will; to do nothing, or in any case indulge our own craving for pleasure or power (Jung, Search, p. 101).

In many of Guido's daydreams he craves pleasure and power simultaneously. This is clearly true in the extended harem fantasy which occurs late in the film. Here Guido dreams that all the women in his life have returned to him to

[11]C. G. Jung, Modern Man in Search of a Soul, trans. W. S. Dell, (New York, 1933), pp. 105-106. Subsequent references will appear in text as (Jung, Search).

serve his every pleasure and satisfy his every desire. He
has total power over them, and when they rebel he is able to
subdue them with relative ease. His efforts, in fact, arouse
a round of applause from his appreciative victims. To a somewhat lesser degree, Guido's desire for pleasure and power is
implicit in his other fantasies as well.

Fellini consistently indicates that Guido's desire to
recapture his youth is motivated by his fear of death. Guido
senses that his masculinity and virility are waning. The
ladies in the harem, for instance, accuse Guido of being
impotent during their rebellion. "What makes him think he's
still young?" asks the French actress, "He's a lousy lover."
We hear another voice add, "Talk and kisses, that's his speed.
Then he goes to sleep." Accordingly, after Guido makes love
to Carla, he immediately falls asleep while she continues to
sit up reading her comic book.

Guido's sense of mortality was developed at a very young
age. It is in evidence as early as the Saraghina episode.
During the sequence in which Guido is punished for his visit
to Saraghina we see a shot of two bare feet inside a glass
coffin. In the background, projected against the wall, we
see Guido's shadow. Once again the silhouette is juxtaposed
to an image of death. We see the boy, in silhouette, put his
hand to his mouth in shock. He runs to the right and crosses
the screen. The camera pans right simultaneously, and, in
the process, moves right across the coffin towards the head

of the figure inside. At the end of the pan, the camera rests
on the face of a mummified saint. Now we see what has horri-
fied the boy. The face of the saint is hideously pockmarked,
for the mummification process has only partially preserved the
body from the ravages of time. The camera then zooms in on
the face for a tight shot which, for the moment that it is
held on the screen, reveals in even greater detail the festering of the face partially eaten away by the slow process
of decay. Once again the silhouette is juxtaposed to an
image of death.

This shot of the moldering saint represents, in the context of the film, Guido's first encounter with death. Guido
is so terrified during the encounter that he runs directly to
the confession booth to presumably unburden his now all-too-
mortal soul of the weight of his sins. Thus, Guido's first
encounter with the grim reality of death and decay is a terrifying experience which is etched forever upon his memory.
The image of the festering saint lurks permanently in the
recesses of his subconsious and emerges in his memories to
haunt him.

The Church

There are, however, other significant elements in the
crisis which Guido experiences in 8-1/2 besides his unwill-
ingness to accept the fact that he is beginning to grow old.
Guido first glimpses the grim reality of death when he gazes

upon the moldering saint at the Catholic school he attends as a boy. The fear of mortality which he experiences for the first time here drives him to seek the solaces of the confessional. Thus, at this moment there is clear relationship between the fear of death and the guilt which the schoolmasters have instilled in him as a result of his clandestine visit to Saraghina. The fear of death drives him to confess his sins, which, in this case, are sexual in nature. Clearly, an equation has been made in his mind between the sin of lust and both the decay of the body and the damnation of the soul after death. As the priest tells him in the confessional, "Saraghina is the devil," and the devil, of course, leads the soul into eternal damnation.

At the end of the episode Guido returns to Saraghina. It is a choice which is to set the moral tone for his entire life. He is willing to risk damnation in some distant and unspecified future in return for the pleasures of the flesh in the present. This is surely the beginning of the process by which Guido rejects, at least in terms of his conscious decisions, the moral authority and the theological doctrines of the Church. Yet, he is unable to escape the sense of guilt with which the priests have conditioned him to respond to his sexual indulgences as a boy. As he enters middle age in 8-1/2, this sense of sexual guilt appears to become quite strong, for, while death and damnation might have seemed quite distant to the boy, they have become an approaching

eality to the man. While he clearly rejects the concept of
damnation as an intellectual proposition and views the Church
with a certain wry sense of irony, as in the steam bath
scene, the fear of damnation has been deeply embedded in his
innermost and least rational feelings and he is unable to
escape it. According to Armando Favazza, ". . . The Jesuits
have always said, 'Give us a child for the first six years;
then, do with him what you will, he will be ours.'"[12] Surely
this is true of Guido. Although he rejects the moral author-
ty of the Church, he has the nagging conscience of a Jesuit.

Moreover, it is significant that Guido is an Italian.
The Church pervades every aspect of Italian life; its influence is inescapable. According to Nicole Zand, in his
article called "Mauvaise Conscience d'une Conscience Chrétienne," Fellini himself has remarked that there are no secu-
lar Italians. "'Il n'y a pas un Italien qui soit laïc, a
avoué Fellini."[13]

This general societal influence is intensified considerably, however, by Guido's particularly harsh Catholic education. As Guido Aristarco puts it in his article, "L'Intellectuel, L'Artiste et le Télépathe":

[12]Armando Favazza, "Fellini: Analyst without Portfolio," Man and the Movies (Baltimore, 1967), p. 184.

[13]Nicole Zand, "Mauvaise Conscience d'une Conscience
Chrétienne," Études Cinématographieques--Federico Fellini*
8-1/2, 28-29 (Hiver, 1963), p. 50. From Le Nouveau Candide,
30-V-1963.

'La Saraghina est l'enfer,' dit à Guido le confe
seur. Cette veille faute continuer d'oppresser Guido
adulte, quadragénaire. Le protagoniste de son film,
ainsi qu'il le dit, a recu une éducation catholique q'
lui crée d'inguérissables complexes.[14]

Throughout 8-1/2 Guido is engaged in the battle to ri

himself of the taboos imposed by his Catholic education.[15]

The struggle begins when Guido, as a boy, first decides to

join his friends in their visit to Saraghina. Visually, tl

first break is represented by a striking overhead shot whi

occurs early in the Saraghina episode. As Guido pauses

momentarily, he is photographed in an overhead shot looking

rather small and insignificant as he stands upon the school

yard far below the camera. In the foreground, a large stat

of a bishop, its back to the camera, presumably on the roof

of the school, looms large across the screen. Its right ar

is raised in a benediction, and Guido, on the ground below,

is framed by the Bishop's head and upraised arm, suggesting

his entrapment by the Church's rigid morality. When Guido

decides to join his friends he runs off to the right of the

screen out from under the Bishop's arm, and certainly this

a rather literal representation of the fact that Guido is n

emerging, for the first time in his life, from the narrow

[14]Guido Aristarco, "L'Intellectuel, L'Artiste, et Le
Telepathe," Etudes Cinématographiques--Federico Fellini*
8-1/2, 28-29 (Hiver, 1963), p. 43.

[15]Fellini speaks of himself in much the same vein when
he discusses the damaging effects of education in "The Long
Interview." See Tullio Kezich and Federico Fellini, "The
Long Interview," Federico Fellini's Juliet of the Spirits,
ed. Tullio Kezich, trans. Howard Greenfeld (New York, 1965)
p. 29.

confines of Catholic morality.

Guido's escape from the Church's authority, however, is only illusory at best. After his brief interlude with Saraghina he is, of course, dragged back to his school by the priests and subjected to a series of humiliating punishments which scar him for the rest of his life, for his teachers attempt to convince him to fear all contact with women. In the dining room, a bearded priest reads aloud about a saint who not only abhorred contact with women but also fled whenever a woman came into his presence. In the confessional booth, a few shots later, the priest asks Guido whether he knew that Saraghina was the devil. By this time, however, Saraghina has become representative, in the teachings of the priests, of all women, so that the priest is really saying that all women are agents of the devil.

Even within the Church, however, Guido is able to find a different and far more positive vision of womanhood. After leaving the confessional booth, Guido kneels before a statue of the Virgin. The face is rather sensual and is reminiscent both of Caterina Boratto, who plays the mystery lady in Guido's hotel, and Claudia Cardinale, who plays Guido's ideal woman. The statue, particularly in terms of its sensuality, suggests that, despite the teachings of the priests at Guido's school, the Catholic faith is fundamentally grounded upon a fairly positive concept of womanhood. Luigi Barzini, for instance, in The Italians, points out the central role

which the Madonna, as the epitome of the self-sacrificing
womanhood, plays in the Italian church:

> The fact that woman is the predominant character of
> Italian life, even if not the most conspicuous, can be
> read in many small signs. Almost as many popular songs
> are dedicated every year to La Mamma as to voluptuous
> hussies or romantic beauties. 'Mamma Mia!' is the most
> common exclamation. What other people call for their
> mother in time of stress or danger? . . . The next most
> common exclamation is 'Madonna,' which is a supernatural
> equivalent, as La Madonna is the universal symbol of
> suffering and self-sacrificing womanhood.
> The Church itself happily encourages this national
> tendency. Jesus Christ shares, in Italy, His supreme
> place with His Mother, on almost equal footing. . . .[16]

This matriarchal element becomes an important aspect of
Guido's desire for women. Throughout the film he longs for
women who will mother him, who will sacrifice their own concerns in order to dedicate themselves completely to his pleasure. This is what Guido is looking for when he returns to
Saraghina, and the point is underscored visually by the fact
that the film dissolves from a close-up of the Virgin's face,
surrounded by candles, looking down towards Guido, to a shot
of the pill box on the beach which serves as Saraghina's
home. When Guido returns to Saraghina he begins his search
for the ideal Madonna figure who will serve him throughout
his life.

During the confessional sequence, then, two faces of the
Church are presented to the audience. The grotesque face of
the embalmed saint is juxtaposed to the statue of the Virgin.

[16]Luigi Barzini, The Italians (New York, 1964), p. 212.

The former seems to epitomize the hysterically repressive
Catholicism of the school, a lifeless and festering morality
which ought to have been buried long ago. The latter represents the forgiving and maternal aspects of Catholicism which
still appeal to Guido. Suzanne Budgen makes this very point
in her study of Fellini:

> The two priests who come chasing after Guido,
> dodging and falling around like knockabout comedians,
> have an incongruity of appearance which suggests in
> comic form a distorted attitude of mind. Seldom has
> organised morality been made to seem so ridiculous. The
> other priests, before whom Guido is haled, are enclosed
> and unnatural. In a room without windows, the prosecu-
> tor, introduced as the last in a line of portraits, is
> only slightly more alive than they, and the strange sex-
> lessness, achieved by using women made up as men, which
> pervades the assembly makes Guido's accusers seem far
> less wholesome than the company they have snatched him
> from.
>   The hideous face of the saint, by whose shrine
> young Guido is seen to kneel, does nothing to cleanse
> the face of organised religion, but the face of the Vir-
> gin recalls that of the vision in the spa and suggests
> that the fascination she has for Guido is that of a
> half-forgotten memory, enhanced with the aura of
> religious mystery.[17]

There is another irony inherent in the image of the dead
saint, for if it momentarily frightens young Guido into
worrying about the state of his soul (after all the priests
have told him that he has committed a mortal sin), it also
suggests that, at least in physical terms, both saints and
sinners meet the same fate after death. It suggests the ultimate absurdity of asceticism and self-denial at least as
strongly as it suggests the necessity of looking to one's

[17]Budgen, pp. 50-51.

soul so that, presumably like the saint, one can transcend
the wasting of the flesh after death.[18]

In any respect, however, the influence of the Church
upon Guido is indisputable. Nicole Zand, in his article
"Mauvaise Conscience d'une Conscience Chrétienne," goes so
far as to suggest that Guido's obsession with sin is the
major theme of 8-1/2:

> Dans ce contexte, le thème le plus apparent du
> scenario: l'obsession de la femme et des femmes, disons
> pour mieux le situer, le thème du 'harem,' se révèle en
> réalité non fondamental. Il est seulement le point
> d'actualisation majeur de ce qui est, chez Fellini,
> véritablement essentiel: l'obsession du péché. . .
> (Zand, pp. 50-51).

Thus Zand does not see 8-1/2 as a film about a man's relationships with the women in his life. Rather, he views this
aspect of the film merely as revealing the major theme, which
concerns a man's relationship with his church and his conscience. He seems to be suggesting that 8-1/2 is the film
about the Catholic conscience in Italy which Daumier says
Guido wants to make as he talks to him following the Saraghina episode. Certainly there seems to be an abundance of
evidence to support this conclusion.

Guido is burdened with a heavy sense of guilt, particularly with respect to his romantic entanglements. Guido's
deep sense of guilt in sexual matters is manifested most

[18]This is particularly true if one accepts Aristarco's
assumption that the mummified saint is identical to the one
who is the subject of the dining hall lecture. See
Aristarco, p. 43.

learly in his relationship with Carla. He desperately
ttempts to hide their affair from his associates, and, in
he process, makes it seem rather sordid and distasteful.
hen Carla visits the spa's nightclub while Guido is there
ith his associates, his embarrassment is acute. He barely
cknowledges the sly glances she casts his way while sitting
lone at the opposite end of the dance floor. Guido's worst
moment, however, comes when Maurice offers to read Carla's
mind. She asks if she can think of a person, and the film
cuts to Guido nervously biting his nails.

All of this is contrasted, in the film, to Mezzabotta's
relationship with Gloria. His affair is open and above-
board. He is clearly motivated by love, however misguided
that love might be. Guido, on the other hand, does not love
Carla, and merely uses her for his sexual pleasure. She
seems to realize this and often asks Guido anxiously if he
really loves her, but her questions are always greeted with
silence.

Despite Guido's affairs the idea of divorce apparently
never enters his mind. Given the fact that Luisa, as shall
be demonstrated later, is truly indispensible to him for
various psychic reasons, as well as the near impossibility of
obtaining a divorce in Italy, the fact that he never seems to
consider it can certainly be ascribed to other factors besides his bourgeois sense of morality.

Guido's sense of guilt, however, certainly motivates his

invitation to Luisa to join him at the spa. Having spent th
evening attempting to ignore the presence of his mistress at
the night club, he is confronted by the accusations of his
wife when he talks to her on the telephone. She says that
she called him twice earlier and pointedly asks where he was.
Typically, Guido lies and says that he was working late at
the production office. He continues to lie to her throughout
the conversation, giving her the impression that he is alone
and working hard. The camera is tightly focused on his guilt
ridden face in close-up, and as he continues to lie it moves
in to scrutinize him even more closely. Suddenly, at the end
he brightens up and asks her to join him, as if the invitation will somehow mitigate his guilt.

Guido's guilt, however, is not totally relieved by this
gesture. After he hangs up the phone, he then goes upstairs
to the production room, impelled by guilt to lend at least
some validity to his story that he has been hard at work all
night.

Guido never seems to suffer any particular pangs of
remorse over the fact that he is not living up to his commit-
ment to make the film. Certainly he experiences a sense of
desperation and frustration as his creative abilities seem to
dry up, but he never seems to experience any sense of guilt
at the enormous waste of men, materials, and money caused by
his equivocation. Only in sexual matters does Guido experience guilt, for, as Zand points out, he has been conditioned

₂ his education to equate sin with forbidden sex (Zand,
. 51).

Despite the central role which sin and guilt play in the
ilm, however, Zand exaggerates considerably when he asserts
hat they constitute the major theme of 8-1/2. Guido's dif-
iculties manifest themselves in terms of his relationships
ith women. Just as his obsession with sin is merely one of
he factors contributing to his spiritual and artistic paral-
sis, so it is only one of the factors contributing to his
nability to establish meaningful relationships with the
romen in his life. To say that it is the focal point of the
ilm is to mistake one detail for the final design.

Paradoxically, in fact, Guido's Catholic education has
₂ade it practically impossible for him to engage in relationships with women that go much deeper than sex. He views
romen as an adolescent, either as sex objects or as possible
representatives of his feminine ideal exemplified by the
statue of the Virgin he prays before as a young boy. One of
Guido's most difficult problems is that he can never proceed
beyond the ideal. In all women he seeks the great Madonna,
pure and idealized, who will sacrifice herself to his every
need.

Guido views the Church's crippling influence on his emotional life bitterly. His vision of the Cardinal in the mud
bath, which he intends to include in his film, is satirical
and derisive. In fact, this portrait of the old and senile

Cardinal seated in a mud bath while babbling Latin banalities, flanked by a priest with an empty smile across his
face, epitomizes Guido's feelings about the Church. It is
anachronism unable to come to grips with the difficulties and
complexity of modern life, and therefore dependent upon out-
moded clichés to uphold its moral authority.

Yet, there is an ironic dimension to Guido's grimly
satirical portrait of the Church as a senile old man spouting
mindless clichés while sitting in a mud bath. Daumier ex-
presses it while talking to Guido in the restaurant of their
hotel after the Saraghina episode. He tells Guido, "You want
to make a serious film about the Catholic conscience in
Italy. . . . But you start out intending to denounce, then
along the way you turn into an accomplice." In other words,
Guido's obsession with the Church, even when he views it in
completely derogatory manner, reveals the extremely strong
grip which the institution has upon his consciousness. Thus
in the very act of denouncing the Church he reveals the
powerful hold it still has upon him.[19]

The Filmmaker's Alienation

The Church's powerful hold on Guido is, thus, manifested
in many aspects of his behavior. The most important of these
is his difficult relationships with women; however, Guido's

[19]Zand argues, in his article on the film, that Guido's
revolt against the Church is really a form of acceptance.
See Zand, p. 50.

ability to relate to women is merely one aspect of his gen-
al alienation from all the people in his world, and from
at world itself. Along with Guido's obsession with old
e, death, and sin, this sense of alienation is one of the
portant stumbling blocks for him to overcome if he is to
eak the bonds of his paralysis.

More than anything else, Guido can be characterized as a
n who uses people rather than relating to them. This is
plicit in the very career he has chosen for himself, that
a film director. The film director, after all, is a man
o must be able to see and use people as objects, as means
carrying out a certain artistic conception.

Significantly, this concept of the director's role is
rticularly characteristic of certain Italian directors,
ch as Fellini and Antonioni. For instance, during the mak-
g of 8-1/2 few of the actors, outside of Mastroianni, had
y idea of the true nature of their parts. Except for Mas-
roianni, few were allowed to read the entire script, and
ften they received their lines only a half hour before
hooting time.[20] In this way Fellini attempted to prevent
hem from developing interpretations of their parts which
iverged from Fellini's own desires.[21]

[20]Boyer, p. 166.

[21]Fellini, during "The Long Interview," speaks of choos-
ng faces rather than actors and then of manipulating them
ike puppets (pp. 42-43). Antonioni is even more extreme and
ften speaks of actors as if they were merely props like so

Thus, the director's relationship with his actors can generally be characterized as a subject-object relationship. They are merely elements or objects to be manipulated by him in order to achieve a specific dramatic effect. It is, therefore, fitting that Guido be cast as a film director of this type, because that profession is merely an extenstion his everyday behavior. Guido manipulates poeple as objects in his work just as he does in every other aspect of his life. This, in fact, is one of Guido's other difficulties; he is unable to relate to others, particularly women, as human beings, but sees them rather as objects to be manipulated, like actors in his films, according to his desires.

This is most explicit, of course, in Guido's fantasies In them he creates a world in which all people are eminentl submissive, and succumb entirely to Guido's will. He constructs his fantasies to suit his desires in much the same way that he directs his films. Here he creates the complia world which eludes him in reality. This is characteristic, for instance, of the harem fantasy and of his making up Car to play parts.[22]

many trees. Michelangelo Antonioni, "A Talk with Michelangelo Antonioni on His Work," L'Aventurra, trans. by Louis Brigante (New York, 1969), pp. 225-226.

[22]Ted Perry suggests that even the camera work in 8-1/ indicates Guido's isolation from his environment. He refer specifically to subjective camera shots in which people sta directly towards the camera identified with Guido. See Ted Perry, "Signifiers," pp. 80-81.

There are two sets of motifs in <u>8-1/2</u> which are representative of Guido's alienation from his world and his tendency to view people as objects. One is the proliferation of
photographs throughout the film. The other is the literal
imposition of barriers between Guido and other people in the
film.

Ted Perry points out the relationship between the numerous photographs in the film and Guido's alienation:

> . . . A film director is inexorably estranged from
> people because he treats them as images, as objects, as
> things he will use and turn into celluloid. The use of
> photographs on Guido's bed is evidence of this treatment
> of people, and certainly when Guido lies down on the
> photographs and sleeps with one propped up on the pillow
> between his legs, these photographs become clear sig-
> nifiers of Guido's 'otherness' from the world and
> people. . . (Perry, "Signifiers," pp. 82-83).

Furthermore, it is no accident that almost all the still
photographs we see in the film are pictures of women, particularly women's faces. Throughout the film Guido's tendency
to regard people as objects impinges most directly upon his
relationships with women, for he envisions women almost exclusively as means of satisfying his desires. Furthermore,
the pictures of women in Guido's room and in his production
office are all photographs of actresses, presumably being
cast for his film. The casting of these actresses, through
their photographs, clearly becomes another means for him to
extend his sexual fantasies into both art and real life. The
placement of the actress's picture between Guido's legs while
he lies in bed enjoying a sexual fantasy merely makes the

erotic undertones of this relationship explicit.

From the beginning of the film, therefore, these pictures are a pervasive part of Guido's environment. At the beginning of the film, as the doctor concludes his examination of Guido, he picks up a picture of an actress from the other bed and asks Guido whether she is American. As he put the picture down and packs his bag, we see that the entire bed is covered with pictures of actresses. Later, when Guid returns to his room after his argument with Conocchia, he does a somersault on top of these same pictures, landing on top of them and crushing them with his body.

Among all these photographs, moreover, there is one which seems to be of particular significance. This is the picture of the actress who is to play the part of Luisa in Guido's film. Her photograph appears four times in the film Her picture appears twice in the production room on two different partitions covered with the pictures of actresses. Although the lower half of the picture is covered by others both times, the strikingly large eyes are unmistakable.

This photograph next appears when he somersaults onto the bed covered with photographs during the scene in which I envisions Claudia in his bedroom. In the center of the bed, half covered by other pictures, but with the distinctive eye still staring outward, is the picture of the actress who wil play the part of the wife in the film. Significantly, the bed on which it lies is the same one which will later be use by Luisa when she joins Guido at the spa.

Later in the film, the picture recurs once more, perhaps in its most striking context. This is in the bedroom scene between Guido and Luisa. At one point she walks over to a dresser and withdraws a small box of pills from her pocket-book which rests atop it. As she turns slightly to open the pillbox, she notices that on the dresser to her right is the picture of the girl who will portray her in Guido's film. All the other pictures, which had earlier covered her bed, have apparently been cleaned out of the room, but this one Guido has saved. She picks up the picture and looks at it more closely. Then she turns for a moment to look suspicious-ly at Guido, who at this point is feigning sleep. She turns back to the dresser, returns the photograph to its place and drinks down her pill.

Of course, the relationship between Luisa and the myste-rious picture is not clarified until the actress appears in the part of Guido's wife during the screen tests. Even in physical terms the actress, apart from the fact that her hair is longer, resembles Luisa. She has the same narrow, angular features. The resemblance is accentuated when Guido in-structs her to put on a pair of glasses. They are identical to the ones Luisa wears. She even talks like Luisa. "I'm offering you your freedom," she says. "You don't need me any more. I'm only in your way." Luisa recognizes the role in-stantly. When asked whom the actress is playing, she answers grimly, "Can't you guess? It's the wife."

The film Guido plans to make is really an extension of his fantasy life; it provides him with the opportunity to re-design his life, to control and manipulate the people in his life in a way which eludes him in reality. In the case of Luisa, this is forshadowed by the fact that Guido keeps a picture of the actress who is to portray her on the dresser rather than her own photograph. There is a particularly poignant quality to all of this, particularly for Luisa. Of all the women in Guido's life, she most effectively maintains her autonomy and she, therefore, feels most deeply violated by the surrogate victory Guido attempts to achieve on the screen.

Curiously enough, Guido is not entirely successful in reducing Luisa to the level of a puppet. Deeply humiliated by the fact that his wife, seated in the audience, must wit-ness this highly uncomplimentary portrayal of herself, Guido whispers to her under his breath, "Luisa, I love you." The actress on the screen glares out toward the audience and seems to reply to him, "You lie with every breath."

Ironically, the sequence is also prophetic. Luisa is so outraged by the portrayal of her on the screen that she, like her fictional counterpart, decides that she will leave Guido. Furious at the public revelation of their most intimate quar-rels, she, like the woman on the screen, accuses Guido of being a liar. Unlike her cinema counterpart, however, she no

longer focuses on his compulsion to lie about his relationships with other women. Instead she now denounces his work
as a lie. The dialogue comes very close, however, to paral-
leling what we have just seen take place on the screen.

The other device which Fellini uses to visually represent Guido's alienation is the imposition of barriers between
people in the film. In particular, people are consistently
photographed, throughout the film, as disappearing behind
barriers and reappearing on the other side. Perry also remarks upon the barrier motif in 8-1/2, at least as it is manifested by the glass box enclosing the fakir and the sheets
which separate Guido from the Cardinal (Perry, "Signifiers,"
p. 82).

The film is studded with other barrier images as well.
When Daumier first enters Guido's bedroom after the nightmare
sequence which begins the film, he enters behind a glass partition decorated with a frosted baroque design incorporating
romantic figures of nudes. Later in the film, when Luisa
enters the bedroom before her argument with Guido, she walks
behind the same glass partition. At Carla's hotel, as she
washes her hands, Guido watches her through a small window in
the wall which separates them. Later, as they eat and she
babbles on about her husband, Guido hides behind a newspaper.
When he later dreams that he is visiting his parents in a
cemetery, he sees his father walking swiftly behind an opening in the cemetery wall. One of the first images in the

farmhouse memory is that of one of the nurses chasing Guido.
As she chases him, she zig-zags in front and behind a series
of sheets hanging from a washline. In the production room,
Guido walks behind two partitions covered with actresses'
photographs. When the site of the rocket launching tower is
visited by Guido and his friends, various members of the
party are shown walking behind screens erected on the set.
Often the lighting in the background projects their shadows
upon these screens. When the entire party mounts the steps
of the tower, they walk behind a screen on the tower, and
their shadows are projected against it.

Perhaps the most compelling manifestation of this barrier motif occurs during the nightmare which opens the film.
Here, the various people in the tunnel, compartmentalized
within their automobiles, are totally oblivious to Guido's
fate as he struggles to free himself from his own car, slowly
filling up with mysterious and deadly vapors. An old man
continues to paw the young girl beside him. A man in a car
next to Guido's turns to stare at him with a cold and almost
clinical air as if he were examining a strange insect trapped
in a bottle. The passengers of a nearby bus hang out the
windows like fresh meat. In the car behind Guido's, a woman
seems totally impassive, but the man leans forward over the
steering wheel, a sadistic leer spread across his face.

Thus, in the automobile tunnel we have a portrait of
Guido's world. It is a world of people completely detached

and isolated from each other. Each car serves as a self-enclosed barrier between Guido and those around him. Each group of passengers is incapable of compassion or of any other emotional relationship with any of their neighbors. Here people do not interact; they merely observe each other.

All of the various barrier images discussed here contribute to the sense of alienation which pervades the film. One final motif deserves at least brief mention in this context, for it too, in a more ironic vein, indicates how the people in Guido's world tend to view each other as objects, often seeing only what they desire to see. Throughout the film various people look into mirrors, and occasionally discover that they reflect others in roles which the viewers have imposed upon them.

For instance, when Guido's mother views him in the reflection of the window of a crypt during the cemetery dream, she sees him as a grown man dressed in a schoolboy uniform, suggesting that she always viewed him as her little boy even after he had grown up. Later in the film, during the press conference fantasy, Guido envisions his wife wearing a bridal veil and dress reflected in the mirrored surface of the table behind which he sits. As the young bride she embodies the ideal of purity and innocence which he seeks in all women. As he looks up, she fades back into the crowd of reporters indicating a recognition on Guido's part that their marriage has broken up and that, beyond this, the dream might be impossible to attain.

Often throughout the film mirrors are disorienting. The reflection of Luisa as bride appears upside down from Guido's point of view, and earlier in the same scene we see an upside down reflection of his producer. During the love scene in Carla's room the camera, at one point, appears to be pointed towards Guido lying in bed when in fact it is photographing only a reflection of him in a mirror on a closet door.

Although Guido looks at himself many times in mirrors throughout the film, only once does he take a long hard look at himself as he really is. The first close-up look at Guido's face occurs when he walks into his bathroom at the beginning of the film, looks into the mirror, and discovers a tired middle-ager. His face is weary and lined and his hair is grey and rumpled. There are heavy bags under his puffy eyes. For one of the few times in the film Guido acknowledges the reality of his condition as he bends down in three stiff movements while holding his back, in comic imitation of a man bent with age. These are the same labored movements which Mezzabotta makes, without the comic intention, when he rises to greet Guido at the spa.

Thus, Guido, who is attempting to rediscover his identity in middle age, catches a brief glimpse of the reality of his condition at the beginning of the film. Generally, however, when Guido looks at himself in a mirror, he sees the mask of the charming and attractive film director which he puts on for the world to see.

The Escapist Impulse

The fact that Guido seldom sees himself as he really is
when he looks into a mirror is indicative of the fact that
his search for identity is not pursued with any consistency.
Often, in fact, he seems more anxious to avoid his difficulties altogether and lapses into a variety of escapist fantasies ranging from dreams to hallucinations.

Although much of this activity is escapist in nature,
not all of it is voluntary. Guido's dreams, for instance,
play a prominent role in the early part of the film. They,
of course, spring directly from the unconscious and are not
subject to Guido's control, as are many of his other fantasies. The film opens, as we have seen, with a terrifying
nightmare in which Guido escapes being gassed to death only
to fall hundreds of feet from the sky into the ocean.

The most important aspect of this dream for our purposes,
however, is the flying motif. This flying motif recurs
throughout the film, in one form or another, and is consistently associated with escape and freedom. Thus, although the
opening nightmare is ultimately a dream of death, it is also,
for a few moments at least, a dream of escape. Guido soars
deliriously into the heavens after being liberated from the
deadly confines of his automobile. Until he discovers that
he is bound by a rope to a man on the beach below, he enjoys
an exhilarating sense of freedom and joy.

Throughout the film, images associated with flying

continue to be evocative of Guido's escapism. In the farmhouse memory, for instance, the little girl makes the flying
motion with her hands when she chants the magic words "ASA
NISI MASA." The word is an anagram for the word "anima," and
during the Jungian section it will become evident that one of
Guido's anima figures is an actress whose name, Claudia
Cardinale, seems to imply a reference to birds. Since the
anima figure is often a vehicle for Guido's escapism, the
reference to birds and flying is appropriate. It is no accident that when Claudia runs towards Guido when she first
appears, Fellini photographs her as if she were floating towards him with her arms swept back like wings.

Throughout the film, many of the women are depicted as
being dressed in feathers. Often this image is also tinged
with irony. For instance, when Claudia, the actress, finally
arrives at the end of the film, she is wearing a huge, black
feathered boa. Her arrival, of course, signals the final
disillusionment for Guido. Furthermore, Jacqueline Bonbon,
Guido's now decrepit first love, most closely resembles, in
her ludicrous bird costume, an obese ostrich.

There are also images of flying in the film which are
less naturalistic. 8-1/2 is studded with references to air-
planes and rockets. The most obvious of these is the rocket
launching tower, which is explicitly linked to the escape
motif.

In Guido's film the survivors of the nuclear holocaust

attempt to flee to another planet. The film, of course, is
another expression of the escapism which characterizes Guido,
this time projected on an epic scale.

Escape is also suggested when Luisa considers having an
affair with Enrico. As they talk on the rocket tower a jet
plane roars overhead. The flying motif is used to underscore
the possibility of escape but this time for her. She too is
tempted momentarily to slip the bonds of her marriage.

This motif recurs at other times throughout the film.
One of Guido's harem girls, for instance, is a stewardess
with whom he apparently dallied while an airplane he was on
was diverted unexpectedly to Copenhagen. Hers is the same
voice we heard in the steam bath announcing that the Cardinal
was expecting Guido to appear for an audience. Guido's daydreams and memories are often cross referential in this way.

Finally, there is the matter of the futuristic painting
of a rocket on its launching pad. As we have seen, it is
found both at the launching site and in the production office
on the wall behind the bed upon which Cesarino's "nieces"
romp. Ted Perry's suggestion that this painting, along with
the launching tower on the beach, is representative of freedom places it neatly within the flying motif:

> . . . The spaceship platform itself is a creature of
> mystery and illusion. Early in the film, as Guido be-
> gins to fly, the platform is associated with that flying
> and is thus linked with a dream world of freedom.
> Dreams, seers, clairvoyants, and magic all represent
> this world of absolute freedom, understanding, and un-
> hindered action toward which Guido aspires. In this

regard, it is interesting to speculate about the
'cousins' in the production office. As these two girls
romp around on the bed, obviously free and uninhibited,
we see them against a picture of the spaceship. In
wanting to be as uninhibited as the girls, Guido aspires
to a world of science fiction, free of the earth, here
and now (Perry, "Signifiers," p. 84).

The motif, of course, also has other more overtly psy-

chological implications when it appears in dreams. In purely

Freudian terms the dream of flying is associated with tumes-

cence, and the euphoria which generally accompanies such

dreams is generally attributed to sexual excitement.[23] The

portion of Guido's dream in which he flies is unquestionably

euphoric.

The association of flying with tumescence is particular-

ly explicit in the brief appearance of the phallic launching

tower in the nightmare. Later in the film, at the end of the

scene in which Guido and his friends have visited the towers,

the producer calls down to Guido from the tower as he stands

below talking to Luisa, "Guido! Are you coming up or not?"

The film then cuts to a shot of Guido in bed, a worried

expression on his face, as if he were concerned about the

same question in a slightly different context.

Guido's dream, however, is a dream of falling as well as

a dream of flying. In a Freudian analysis, falling, as a

dream experience, is associated with anxiety rather than

---

[23]Sigmund Freud, A General Introduction to Psychoanalysis, trans. by Joan Riviere (New York, 1924), p. 162.

uphoria, detumescence rather than sexual arousal. Jung suggests that the dream might also reveal self-destructive and uicidal drives and provide a temporary outlet for them.[24] his line of reasoning seems particularly relevant to Guido's ondition. Not only does he clearly exhibit self-destructive endencies, throughout the film, but also these tendencies ulminate explicitly in his dream of suicide at the end of he press conference fantasy.

Dreams, however, are not the only form of escapist fanasy that arises spontaneously in Guido's mind. Guido is also subject to escapist hallucinations which, like his dreams, seem to arise spontaneously from within his subconscious. Specifically, this is characteristic of the appearnces of the vision of Claudia. Seldom does her presence seem to be summoned up consciously by Guido. In the garden, for instance, when he spots her while standing in line at the fountain, his face registers a genuine look of surprise.

Guido, however, does experience memories and fantasies or daydreams which are consciously summoned up. There are two memory episodes in the film, both drawn from Guido's childhood. In both cases women, whether the nurses at the farmhouse or Saraghina, play important roles. Their continual presence in Guido's memories suggests the central role which women have had in shaping Guido's development. In this

[24]Carl Jung, Man and His Symbols (New York, 1964), p. 34.

respect, both episodes are essentially memories of various women who inhabited Guido's childhood.

Most of Guido's fantasies also seem to be about women in one sense or another. As products of Guido's imagination they are even more subject to his conscious control than are his memories, which, however much they may have altered with the time in Guido's mind, are still dependent upon events as they actually occurred in the past. One always has the feeling that Guido directs his fantasies much as he directs his films, and since both are essentially products of his imagination, perhaps there is not really much difference between them. As products of the escapist impulse, these fantasies allow Guido to reorder the difficult world in which he lives so that it conforms to his desires.

Interestingly, dreams and memories seem to predominate in the early part of the film, only to be superseded by a raft of fantasies as it moves towards its conclusion. The importance of women in the fantasies is established from the start, for the first extended fantasy in the film is the one in which Claudia appears in Guido's bedroom to console him after his argument with Conocchia. While it is true that the second extended fantasy is that of Guido's audience with the Cardinal in the mud bath, even this fantasy begins with the sound of a woman's voice, namely the voice of the airline stewardess we later meet in the harem fantasy.

The harem fantasy is concerned exclusively with Guido's

women and his relationship with them. Guido first imagines
an amicable meeting of Luisa and Carla, and this short episode then gives way to the more grandiose harem fantasy in
which all the women in Guido's life are reconciled.

The next significant extended fantasy occurs at the end
of the piazza scene, which itself contains the short halluci-
nation-fantasy of Claudia, the muse, descending into the
courtyard. The arrival of the producer and his entourage and
their announcement of the morning press conference triggers
Guido's own press conference fantasy. While this fantasy
episode ostensibly has little to do with Guido's relationship
with women, two of its most poignant moments reflect this
theme. The first occurs when Luisa, dressed in her wedding
gown, tells him that she wants a divorce, and the second
occurs when he imagines his mother calling to him in the last
moment before he blows his brains out.

Finally, of course, we have the climactic reconciliation
fantasy. Although Guido is reconciled with all the people in
his life, the fantasy is directed chiefly towards an imagined
reconciliation between Guido and his wife. It is this initial
reconciliation which initiates the climactic dance which concludes the film. Moreover, this fantasy is more explicitly
directed by Guido than any of the others. Here he stands in
the center of the circus ring, bullhorn in hand, and literally directs the activities of the participants.

Thus, it is significant that most of Guido's fantasies

and daydreams, as we have seen in this brief summary, relate
in one way or another to his relationship with women. The
predominance of female figures throughout so much of his fan
tasy life, not to mention his memories and dreams (note for
instance the transformation of his mother into his wife in
the cemetery dream), suggests that the female figure is
really the key to his consciousness. The next section will
demonstrate how the predominance of women in his fantasies i
directly related to all of his difficulties: his fear of ol
age and death, his oppressive sense of guilt, his alienation
from the world and the people around him, and his lack of
self-knowledge. If he is to resolve any of these problems i
the film, he ultimately must do so by coming to terms with
these female figures embedded in his consciousness.

CHAPTER III

8-1/2: AN ARCHETYPAL ANALYSIS

I. THE ANIMA

It would not be an exaggeration to suggest that in
Guido's fantasies and memories we find recorded the growth of
one man's sexuality. In his interior world we are introduced
to all the women who have ever influenced Guido, a group
which appears to include all the women he has ever known or
hoped to have known. We meet his mother and nurses who
mothered him as a boy. We come to know Saraghina, who introduced him to sexuality, and Jacqueline Bonbon, with whom he
had his first sexual experience. Both Luisa and Carla reappear in his fantasy world. Apart from these women who have
played a major role in Guido's life, a host of women whom he
has only know, briefly drift in and out of his dream world.
We meet everyone from a stewardess with whom he had a brief
affair in Copenhagen to an actress whom he has promised a
small part in his next film. We even see, in the harem fantasy, the mysterious woman whom Guido finds so alluring in
the hotel but whom he never meets.

Thus, we see the growth of Guido's sexuality, not in
terms of its chronological development, but rather in terms

97

of his relationship with the various women who converge in his imagination and memories, particularly in respect to the harem fantasy. They have never left him, but rather remain as an ongoing and operative part of his consciousness.

The central role which these women assume in Guido's mental life suggests that their importance transcends the commonplace reflections of a middle-aged man upon his past. In order to deal with the predominance of the female in Guido's psyche, it is now necessary to go beyond a contextual reading of the film. The proliferation of females in Guido's consciousness, and their relationship to his personal development is clearly archetypal. Specifically, they conform exactly to descriptions of the anima projection. To examine the anima, therefore, is not to go outside the film, but rather to explore completely the references within it.

The anima is the female component of the male psyche. M. L. von Franz describes the anima in the following manner:

> The anima is a personification of all feminine psychological tendencies in a man's psyche, such as vague feelings and moods, prophetic hunches, receptiveness to the irrational, capacity for personal love, feeling for nature, and--last but not least--his relation to the unconscious. . . .[1]

It is vital to understand that the anima figure is a personification of all these feminine aspects of the male psyche. The anima is, therefore, no mere abstraction. She

[1] M. L. von Franz, "The Process of Individuation," Man and His Symbols (New York, 1964), p. 186.

appears both in male dreams and fantasies. Of course, the
anima is personified as a female figure. The women who
inhabit the dreams and fantasies of men are anima figures,
projections of the feminine aspects of their psyches.

The anima figure, however, does not always remain confined to fantasies and dreams. If a man fails to come to
grips with and understand the nature of his anima it will
emerge from his dreams and fantasies to be projected upon
women in the real world. A man will often become attracted
to a woman because he projects his anima figure upon her:

> All these aspects of the anima have the same tend-
> ency that we have observed in the shadow: That is, they
> can be projected so that they appear to the man to be
> the qualities of some particular woman. It is the pres-
> ence of the anima that causes a man to fall suddenly in
> love when he sees a woman for the first time and knows
> at once that this is 'she.' In this situation, the man
> feels as if he has known this woman intimately for all
> time; he falls for her so helplessly that it looks to
> outsiders like complete madness (von Franz, p. 191).

This tendency of men to cast their anima projections
outward upon the world can have an alienating effect. It
leads them to see the world, not as it is, but rather in
terms of the preconceived images they project upon it. Moreover, this tendency is particularly dangerous because it is
an unconscious, rather than a conscious function of the mind,
so that the subject's awareness of the basis for his alienation is minimized:

> Let us suppose that a certain individual shows no
> inclination whatever to recognize his projections. The
> projection-making factor then has a free hand and can
> realize its object--if it has one--or bring about some

other situation characteristic of its potency. . . .
    The effect of projection is to isolate the subject
from his environment, since instead of a real relation
to it there is now only an illusory one. Projections
change the world into the replica of one's own unknown
face. In the last analysis, therefore, they lead to an
autoerotic or autistic condition in which one dreams a
world whose reality remains forever unattainable. . . .[2]

This is precisely the type of alienation which Guido

exhibits throughout the film. He is unable to relate to the

women in his life as individual human beings because he uncon-

sciously projects his anima upon them and thus perceives them

in terms of a false and idealized image. When these women

fail to measure up to his projection, as in the case of

Claudia, he is bitterly disappointed. His alienation from

the world at large is an extension of this process.

    Guido's anima projections seem to be at the root of most

of his other problems as well. As we shall soon see, there

is a direct relationship between Guido's inability to cope

with middle age and his anima projections. Moreover, Guido's

creative blockage can also be traced to this same source.

His weakness and vacillation are all characteristic of his

anima projection.

    In order for Guido to surmount all of these personal

difficulties he must first come to terms with his anima. He

must raise his projections to the level of consciousness so

that he can confront and understand them, so that he will no

---

[2]C. G. Jung, "Aion," Psyche & Symbol (Garden City,
1958), p. 8. Subsequent references will appear in the text
as Jung, "Aion."

longer be misled by them. Only when Guido becomes conscious

of the nature of his anima projections and reconciles himself

to them will he be able to break the bonds of his paralysis

and alienation. As Edward C. Whitmont puts it:

> Through actualizing the never-before-encountered
> inferior function, anima integration eases the pressure
> of affect-tensions, depressions, moods and 'states,' and
> opens the way to genuine relatedness by virtue of a bet-
> ter ability to see the other person as he or she really
> is. For to the extent that the anima qualities are con-
> sciously experienced they are no longer subject to that
> sort of projection which distorts our view of the other
> person's reality.[3]

For Guido, the integration of his anima projections is neces-

sary if he is to learn how to give love as well as to receive

it.

The integration of projections, such as the anima, and

the unification of the self is the goal of the process of

personal development which Jung calls individuation:

> Individuation means becoming a single homogeneous
> being and, in so far as 'individuality' embraces our
> innermost, last, and incomparable uniqueness, it also
> implies becoming one's own self. We could therefore
> translate individuation as 'coming to selfhood' or
> 'self-realization.'[4]

Jung's theory of psychoanalysis is predicated upon the belief

that individuation, the attainment of psychic wholeness,

should be the ultimate goal of all people.

[3]Edward C. Whitmont, The Symbolic Quest (New York,
1960), p. 199.

[4]C. G. Jung, Two Essays on Analytical Psychology, Col-
lected Works trans. R. F. C. Hull (New York, 1953), p. 173.
Subsequent references will appear in the text as Jung, Two
Essays.

Guido's anima projections are characteristically those
of a middle-aged man. Many of the female figures who inhabit
Guido's thoughts are drawn from his past, a typical syndrome
of middle age. What Guido really desires is a return to the
simple pleasures and innocence of childhood, and this desire,
always implicit in his choice of women, becomes explicit in
his memories and daydreams. He fantasizes a harem, for instance, in the setting of the farmhouse of his boyhood memories. Here all the women he has ever known live together
under one roof and devote themselves, like the nurses he recalls from his boyhood, totally to Guido's happiness. Like
the nurses, they even bathe and dry him.

The important thing to remember, however, about these
pleasant, seductive anima visions is that they are fundamentally alienating. Pleasant as they are, they alienate Guido
from the reality of others. Claudia's real personality, for
instance, differs radically from the anima projection cast
upon her. Guido is bitterly disappointed in the real Claudia
when she appears. If Guido is to relate to other people in
terms of their real personalities, he must first learn to
recognize his anima projections and come to terms with them
so that he will no longer be misled.

It would not be an exaggeration to say that 8-1/2 is
structured, at least in part, upon this process. In the
early part of the film we perceive Guido's alienation from
his world. As the film proceeds, the effects of that

alienation upon the people around him is manifested, and
Guido grows increasingly bitter and disillusioned. His wife
leaves him. Claudia refuses to conform to his preconceptions. He finds that he will be unable to make his film.
The cumulative effect of these blows finally forces Guido to
confront and recognize the fact that he has been misled by
his anima projections and to recognize that he must extend
love to others as well as receive it. Thus, the entire film
is structured around a process of personal development identical to the process of individuation.

This is by no means an insight imposed upon the film
from without. In fact, there are explicit, unmistakable references to the individuation process throughout 8-1/2. The
most significant of these references, perhaps, lies in the
appearance of the word "anima" as a magic word imbedded within Guido's memory. The magic word "ASA NISI MASA," which
plays such a key role in Guido's memories, is none other than
the word "anima" transformed, by the process of a children's
game similar to pig Latin, into a mysterious chant invoking
quasi-occult powers.[5]

The magic word, "ASA NISI MASA," is a vital key to an
understanding of the entire film. Should anyone doubt its
archetypal associations, Fellini provides us with a second
clue which, once again, points directly towards Jung. The

[5]Boyer, p. 24.

name of Maurice's telepathic assistant, who is actually the
one to read Guido's mind, is Maya. Significantly, Maya is
the name of an Eastern goddess with whom Jung associates what
he calls "the projection-making factor." Moreover, Jung
relates this projection-making factor specifically to the
anima projection in the section of <u>Aion</u> entitled "The Syzygy:
Anima and Animus":

> What, then, is this projection-making factor? The
> East calls it the 'Spinning Woman'--Maya, who creates
> illusion by her dancing. Had we not long since known it
> from the symbolism of dreams, this hint from the Orient
> would put us on the right track: the enveloping,
> embracing, and devouring element points unmistakably to
> the mother, that is, to the son's relation to the real
> mother, to her image, and to the woman who is to become
> a mother for him. His Eros is passive like a child's;
> he hopes to be caught, sucked in, enveloped, and de-
> voured. He seeks, as it were, the protecting, nourish-
> ing, charmed circle of the mother, the condition of the
> infant released from every care, in which the outside
> world bends over him and even forces happiness upon him.
> No wonder the real world vanishes from sight.
> If this situation is dramatized, as the unconscious
> usually dramatizes it, then there appears before you on
> the psychological stage a man living regressively, seek-
> ing his childhood and his mother, fleeing from a cruel
> world which denies him understanding. Not infrequently
> a mother appears beside him who apparently shows not the
> slightest concern that her little son should become a
> man, but who, with tireless and self-immolating effort,
> neglects nothing that might hinder him from growing up
> and marrying. You behold the secret conspiracy between
> mother and son, and how each helps the other to betray
> life (Jung, "Aion," pp. 9-10).

Not only is there a character named Maya in the film,
but also, like the Oriental goddess, she is a magician.
Moreover, in the film, as in the passage from Jung, Maya is
associated with the projection-making factor and specifically

ith the anima projection, for the word which she withdraws
rom Guido's mind is a minor alteration of the word "anima."
oreover, her magic act leads directly to Guido's memory of
he women at the farmhouse of his youth who serve as the
odel for his later anima projections. The fact that the
agic word "ASA NISI MASA" is drawn from the farmhouse memory
nly serves to underscore the fact that it is here that his
nima projections originate.

Significantly, in this regard, Maurice, the magician,
lso initiates the reconciliation fantasy which concludes the
ilm. Standing beside Guido's car, he signals the fantasy to
egin with a wave of his hand. Then he orders the lights
round the circus ring to be turned on. He greets people as
hey enter the circle and shows them to their places on the
im. Finally, he leads the chain dance around the perimeter.
f Maya is representative of the projection-making factor,
ertainly he embodies the magical power of the imagination.

There is one further implication of the name Maya which
lso seems relevant to the context of 8-1/2. According to
Jung, Maya is the name of Buddha's mother, and thus she takes
n the aspect of an archetypal mother figure. Furthermore,
he points to similarities, both mythological and etymologi-
cal, between Maya, mother of Buddha, and Mary, mother of
Jesus:

The phonetic connection between G. Mar, F. mere, and the various words for 'sea' (Lat. mare, G. Meer, F. mer) is certainly remarkable, though etymologically accidental. Maybe it perhaps points back to the 'great primordial image' of the mother, who was once our only world and later became the symbol of the whole world? Goethe says of the Mothers that they are 'thronged round with images of all creation.' Even the Christians could not refrain from reuniting their mother of God with the water: 'Ave maris stella' are the opening words of a hymn to Mary. It is probably significant that the infantile word ma-ma (mother's breasts) is found in all languages, and that the mothers of two religious heroes were called Mary and Maya. . . .[6]

All of this is relevant to 8-1/2 in two respects. The anima, for one thing, is essentially a maternal figure, and, for another, she is clearly associated with the Virgin Mary in the film. Guido seeks an element of divinity and perfection in his women. The association of Maya's name with the magic word "ASA NISI MASA" once again serves to reinforce this point.

She also assumes another function in Guido's psychic life. Specifically, she functions as Guido's muse. As she puts it, while lying in bed, "I want to create order, I want to create cleanliness. . . ." Art, after all, is essentially an ordering of reality. The role of the anima as muse is described by M.-L. von Franz in Man and His Symbols:

> But what does the role of the anima as guide to the inner world mean in practical terms? This positive function occurs when a man takes seriously the feelings, moods, expectations, and fantasies sent by his anima and when he fixes them in some form--for example, in writing, painting, sculpture, musical composition, or dancing.

[6]C. G. Jung, Symbols of Transformation, Volume I, trans. by R. F. C. Hull (New York, 1956), p. 251.

When he works at this patiently and slowly, other more
deeply unconscious material wells up from the depths and
connects with the earlier material. . . (von Franz,
p. 195).

When Claudia appears in Guido's bedroom after his argument with Conocchia, she appears in the capacity of his muse.
He enters the room worrying that his creative talent really
has dried up. When he sees Claudia in the room, however, he
regains at least some of his confidence. He soon begins to
speculate upon how he will use her in the film. Her presence
has the effect of renewing the creative impulse within him.

The manner in which Guido projects his anima upon the
other women in his life is most clearly revealed in the harem
episode. Not only is the source of these projections implicit in the setting and action of the episode, but the consequences of these projections is also equally clear. It is
this scene which unequivocably suggests that his anima projections are derived from the women who cared for him at the
farmhouse, and that he therefore imposes characteristics he
associates with them, specifically their willingness to love
and mother him while demanding nothing in return, upon the
women he admires.

Claudia's absence is particularly indicative of the
nature of the harem, for it suggests that rather than focusing his anima projection upon a single projection of the
ideal woman Guido has expanded it here so that it encompasses
all the women he has known. Moreover, the fantasy is little

more than an explicit rendering of the way in which Guido's
mind works in everyday life. He was, in fact, initially
attracted to all of these women because he imposed upon them
the anima projection of the totally submissive female derived
from his youth. The absurdity of their complete subservience
to him in the harem only serves to illustrate how absurdly
his anima projections diverge from reality and, therefore,
alienate Guido from the true nature of the women in his life.
The women in the harem become little more than caricatures of
Guido's deepest desires.[7]

Among all Guido's women only Carla seems even to approach
his ideal of the submissive woman in real life. She exists
mainly to serve Guido's sexual appetite. But even she makes
demands upon him. Instinctively recognizing the nature of
their relationship, she often asks for some indication that

[7]This process of projecting elements from the past into
his fantasies also conforms to the mechanics of the daydream
as described by Sigmund Freud, ". . . The relation of phan-
tasies to time is altogether of great importance. One may
say that a phantasy at one and the same moment hovers between
three periods of time--the three periods of ideation. The
activity of phantasy in the mind is linked up with some cur-
rent impression, occasioned by some event in the present,
which had the power to rouse an intense desire. From there
it wanders back to the memory of an early experience, generally belonging to infancy, in which this wish was fulfilled.
Then it creates for itself a situation which is to emerge in
the future, representing the fulfillment of the wish--this is
the day-dream or phantasy, which now carries in it traces
both of the occasion which engendered it and of some past
memory. So past, present, and future are threaded, as it
were, on the string of the wish that runs through them all."
Sigmund Freud, Character and Culture (New York, 1963), p. 38.

Guido really loves her. Guido, of course, ignores her. Furthermore, she continually badgers Guido about giving her husband a job.

Lest there be any doubt that the harem sequence is archetypal in design, Fellini provides us with a direct reference
to the word "ASA NISI MASA," previously associated with the
farmhouse memory. When Guido is lying in the bath barrel
full of suds, we see him cross his arms and flap his hands in
the same flying motion that the girl in the farmhouse makes
when she chants the words "ASA NISI MASA" at night. The visual reference underscores the fact that the scene illustrates
the operation of the anima principle.

The bath, of course, is an extension of the wine bath
which Guido is forced to take by the nurses when he is a boy.
Beyond this there is a chain of associations with water which
links all of the most important women upon whom Guido projects his anima. Claudia, for instance, offers Guido a glass
of mineral water when he first sees her at the spa. Later,
when the real Claudia arrives, he has her drive to a piazza
which is near the springs. Then as they drive to the piazza
in the car, he tells her that she is to play the part of a
girl whom his protagonist meets at the springs. "She gives
him water to heal him," he says.

Mythologically, of course, water is traditionally the
female element. In particular, the sea is often associated
with the goddess Venus, a fact which Fellini makes use of in

Juliet of the Spirits. Beyond this rather obvious association, however, water also seems to be equated with salvation
in the film, as is suggested by Guido's description of
Claudia's role in his film.

Other women are also associated with water besides
Claudia. Guido is literally offered a drink (although probably not of water) by the French actress when she attempts to
seduce Guido. Guido gives Carla a drink of water when she is
sick. Luisa takes a glass of water to swallow her pills at
night. When Carla enters the restaurant the next morning,
Luisa is there with Rosella drinking a glass of water. This
scene, of course, leads ultimately to the harem scene where
Guido is bathed. The harem scene concludes with Luisa on her
knees contentedly scrubbing the floor, a bucket of water
beside her.

Saraghina, of course, is also associated with water,
specifically with the sea. Her house, which appears to be an
abandoned pill box, is located on a beach. As was pointed
out earlier, there is a direct mythological association between the sea and Venus. Saraghina, perhaps, appears as a
grotesque caricature of the goddess.

In this context it is significant that Guido is plunged
into the sea at the end of the opening nightmare. Juxtaposed
to this image of disaster in the sea are subtle hints of the
presence of Guido's various anima figures. The first and
most blatant of these occurs while Guido is trapped in the

automobile tunnel at the beginning of the nightmare. As
Guido's car fills up with fumes, the film cuts to a shot of a
car in which an old man in white aggressively paws a younger
girl in a low-cut white dress decorated with feathers. As he
paws the girl she writhes in her seat with obvious sexual
excitement. The most striking feature of this shot is that
the girl in the car is Carla.

The next reference to one of Guido's anima figures
occurs somewhat later in the dream, and with far greater sub-
lety. As Guido is floating through the sky, we see for a
moment a shot of the rocket launching tower superimposed upon
the clouds in a double exposure, emphasizing the jagged matrix of pipework near its top. The appearance of the tower
is rather mysterious. Near the end of the film, however, the
identical shot recurs. After Guido's imagined suicide the
camera pans the launching towers. The shot of the second
tower is identical to the one which appears in Guido's nightmare. Is the shot then a premonition of Guido's ultimate
failure, an interpretation which is reinforced by the fact
that Guido's nightmare culminates in the disasterous fall
into the ocean?

A more intriguing alternative presents itself, however.
The glimpse of the tower recalls a similar shot which occurs
during the Saraghina episode. In the midst of her dance the
camera lingers on a shot of a jagged hole in the wall of the
abandoned building in front of which she has been dancing.

It is filled with what appear to be broken reeds, criss-
crossed in every direction. The crisscross pattern of the
reeds bears a strong resemblance to the complex matrix of
pipes at the top of the launching tower, the part of the
tower which Guido sees in his dream.

Fellini, moreover, makes a particular effort to draw our
attention to the pattern of the reeds. He does not cut
directly away from the shot of the hole in the wall, but
rather lingers on it for an extraordinarily long time. Significantly, beyond the matrix of the reeds, the sea rolls
onto the beach. Fellini then focuses our attention upon the
reeds even more by changing the focus of the lens slightly so
that the reeds, which before were somewhat hazy in the picture, now come into sharp relief. He wants the viewer to
notice the pattern of the reeds, and the shot is held still a
while longer before he finally cuts away.

The juxtaposition of the reeds to the sea suggests that
somehow this design is a reference to the anima principle.
Water is emblematic of the anima figure throughout the film,
and certainly Saraghina represents an important aspect of his
anima projection. Given the fact, then, that the shot of the
reeds is given a special emphasis in the Saraghina episode,
and that it closely resembles the structure of the launching
tower as it appears in the nightmare, it becomes clear that
the launching tower in the dream is a direct reference to the
anima principle in general and to Saraghina in particular.

Thus, the appearance of the tower in the dream represents the presence of a second anima figure.

A few moments later the third reference to one of Guido's women occurs in the dream. The man on horseback who appears in the dissolve which ends the shot of the launching tower rides up to a man who is lying face down on the beach with a rope in his hand. Guido is floating at the end of the rope like a kite, and at the horseman's signal the man on the beach yanks on the rope and he plunges into the sea. The significant thing about this episode, in terms of our present discussion, is that the horseman is Claudia's agent. Later in the film he is in the hotel lobby badgering Guido about Claudia's part in the film. Moreover, the man on the beach who pulls Guido down is introduced later in the film as Claudia's press agent. The two of them accost Guido when he returns to the screening room after the argument with his wife. Characteristically, the agent whispers to Guido, "Don't try to hide. We'll always find you." Then Claudia's press agent approaches. "I'm Claudia's press agent," he says, "I met you fifteen years ago. Do you remember me?" Guido nods affirmatively. Ironically, of course, Guido is being quite truthful, since the man apparently still inhabits his night-mares. The presence of both these men in the opening sequence of the film constitutes the third reference to one of Guido's anima figures, namely Claudia. This reference, however, is a most curious one, for it seems to point to

qualities associated with her which are rather destructive.
Her agents who hound Guido throughout the film become his
killers in the dream.

The reference to three of Guido's women in the opening
nightmare suggests the extent to which his anima figures per
vade his subconscious mind. In the dream they emerge both i
representative forms, as does Carla, and in symbolic forms,
as does Saraghina. The opening nightmare is really about
Carla, Saraghina, and Claudia.

The fact that Guido projects his anima upon all these
women reveals the basic factor which unites all of them, at
least in Guido's mind. In this respect, for instance, the
nurses seem to flow into the figure of Saraghina who merges
somewhat with Carla. There seems to be an evolution from on
woman to the next in Guido's mind which unites them all.[8]

In the film, Guido projects the prostitute aspect of hi
anima upon Carla. There is a clear line of development between Saraghina and her. When Guido and Carla are washing u
in the restaurant of her hotel, for instance, we hear in the
background the faint sound of a woman humming Saraghina's
theme, a tune which can only exist, as was explained earlier,
in Guido's mind. It indicates that he projects precisely
those aspects of the anima derived from Saraghina upon Carla
This becomes most explicit in the bedroom scene, when Guido

[8]Guido Aristarco also finds that all of these women
resemble each other and the nurses (Aristarco, pp. 40-46).

makes up Carla's face so that she looks like a prostitute.
When he asks her to pretend she is a whore, he is really asking her to play the role of Saraghina. After he completes
his work, he asks her to smile like a whore. She turns to
the camera and smiles in a heavily lecherous style which she
apparently regards as seductive. The smile becomes emblematic of the prostitute. In fact, Saraghina also smiles in an
identical manner just before dancing off camera to reveal the
hole in the wall behind her filled with reeds.

It is therefore fitting that during the screen tests the
actresses who play Saraghina seem to merge with the ones who
play Carla in a kind of phantasmagoria. Upon Guido's return,
after the argument with Luisa, one of the first tests we see
is that of an actress being cast for the part of Saraghina.
The actress sits down and as the camera moves in for a tight
shot of her face we hear the sound of a young boy's voice.
The boy calls to her in lines reminiscent of the Saraghina
episode, "Saraghina, look. We have money." The word "money"
continues to reverberate throughout the screen tests. Finally near the end of the montage of tests, amidst the whirl-
ing bishops and waving fans, there is a shot of one of the
actresses auditioning for the part of Carla. As she walks
towards the camera, photographed in a close-up, we can hear
the voice of a young boy in the background once again calling,
"Money! Saraghina! Money!" The juxtaposition of these
words to the picture of Carla serves to identify her with

11

Saraghina as well as with the role of the prostitute.

By now it is clear that Guido's ideal woman, whether prostitute or servant, must be one who is willing to extend love while expecting none in return. Guido seeks this quality in his women because he is incapable of love himself. This inability to love is the basis for his emotional paralysis and of his alienation from the world.

This is stated explicitly in the film at the end of Guido's conversation in the piazza with Claudia. Guido has described to her his autobiographical film in which the protagonist, identical to himself, meets a young girl who could be his salvation, to be played by Claudia, and then rejects her. Claudia objects to the character of the protagonist. "This man you describe who doesn't love anyone . . . ," she says, "Why should he expect anything from others?" Guido, o course, is annoyed by her biting questions but he is unable to answer them satisfactorily.

"I really don't understand," she continues. "This man meets a girl who could be his salvation. But he rejects her." Guido replies, "Because he doesn't believe it." At this point Claudia strikes again to the heart of the matter. "Because he doesn't know how to love," she answers. Guido now becomes defensive. He desperately tries to defend the character of his protagonist, because in doing so he is defending himself. "Because no woman can change a man," he answers. Claudia reaffirms her original statement, "Because

doesn't know how to love." Becoming more frustrated by
er insistence upon this point Guido answers again, "And be-
ause I don't want to film another lie." "He doesn't know
ow to love," Claudia replies. It is this inability to love
hich Guido must overcome if he is to break the bonds of his
motional paralysis.[9]

So far the anima figure seems to embody only positive
ttributes. There is another, darker side, however, to the
nima figure. Perhaps the fact that the presence of Claudia's
gents play a destructive role in Guido's nightmare hints at
his darker and more dangerous aspect of the anima figure.
his negative anima figure within Guido's psyche is even a
ore powerful force in shaping his life than is the positive
nima we have so far described.

M.-L. von Franz's description of some of the effects of
he negative anima seems particularly relevant to Guido's
ilemma:

[9]Other writers have commented on this aspect of Guido's
ersonality. Suzanne Budgen, for instance, in commenting
pon the piazza scene, points out that, ". . . When Guido
onfides to Claudia his weariness, his fragmentation, and asks
hy he could not take the healing water of salvation that was
ffered him, Claudia says it is all because he does not know
ow to love, and indeed throughout the film we have seen
uido being loved by others but not loving in return, just as
e have seen him attacked but not attacking" (Budgen, p. 63).
s Dwight McDonald puts it, ". . . he is still, in middle
ge, trying to square the sexual circle: to possess without
eing possessed, to take without giving" (McDonald, p. 19).

In its individual manifestation the character of a
man's anima is as a rule shaped by his mother. If he
feels that his mother had a negative influence on him,
his anima will often express itself in irritable,
depressed moods, uncertainty, insecurity, and touchi-
ness. . . . Within the soul of such a man the negative
mother-anima figure will endlessly repeat this theme:
'I am nothing. Nothing makes any sense. With others
it's different, but for me . . . I enjoy nothing.'
These 'anima moods' cause a sort of dullness, a fear of
disease, of impotence, or of accidents. The whole of
life takes on a sad and oppressive aspect. Such dark
moods can even lure a man to suicide, in which case the
anima becomes a death demon. . . (von Franz, pp. 186-
187).

Throughout the film Guido's behavior is characterized by de-
pression, insecurity and uncertainty. He seems to enjoy
nothing; even sex with Carla must be preceded by a charade if
it is to really interest him. Nothing seems very valuable to
him, and his boredom is all too apparent. Finally, at the
end of the film, when his former escape mechanisms have
failed him, he dreams of suicide.

It is essential to note the fundamental importance which
von Franz, as well as other psychologists, ascribe to the
mother in the formulation of the anima projection. Little
has been said so far about the influence of Guido's mother
upon his anima projections. While other women who perform a
significant role in one's childhood can serve as the basis
for anima projections, the mother remains the major influence
Guido's mother certainly does not fit into the mold of the
positive anima. Rather than serving him selflessly, she seem
to be among the most oppressive elements in his world. In
particular, she allows herself to be used as a tool by the

iests as they attempt to impose upon Guido an oppressive
nse of guilt for his visit to Saraghina. She refuses to
mfort him and, in fact, waves him away with her hand, sob-
ng in words which echo those of the priests, "Oh, Lord,
at shame." This is followed by a close-up in which she
oks with one eye over her handkerchief to see if she has
de the proper impression. Her eye is dry. The entire
rformance has been a sham.

Moreover, Guido's mother is at least partly responsible
r Guido's latent adolescence. When Guido visits her in the
metery dream he is dressed in his schoolboy costume even
ough he is still a middle-aged man. This is a reflection
 the fact that Guido's mother, in the dream, still sees him
d treats him like a little boy. The implication seems to
 that Guido's mother has never really wanted him to grow
, and the fact that she apparently has always treated Guido
 a little boy is responsible, to some degree, for his tend-
cy to view the world from that perspective.

This theme recurs at the end of the film when Guido fan-
sizes his suicide. Just before he pulls the trigger we see
is mother standing on the beach alone calling out to him,
here are you running to, you wretched boy?" Although she
ews him as a boy, she does not mother him like the women at
e farmhouse. Rather, she judges him like the priests at
e seminary. In later life her presence is still felt in
is sense of inadequacy and ineffectualness, as well as in

his dependence on others.

Clearly, if his mother were to serve as the basis for an anima figure, it would be far different from the one which arises from the nurses. If one examines the film to determine whether any character can be found upon whom Guido projects the kind of anima figure that would be derived from his relationship with his mother, the answer is readily apparent. At the end of the cemetery dream, Guido's mother spreads her arms to embrace him for a farewell kiss. He kisses her lightly on the cheek and then she begins to kiss him passionately on the lips. Guido pulls away from her annoyed, but as they part Guido's mother has been transformed into another younger woman dressed in his mother's clothes. Her identity, however, is soon revealed. "Poor Guido," she says, "you must be tired. Do you want to go home?" She pauses but Guido does not answer. She continues, "I'm Luisa, your wife. Don't you recognize me?"

The meaning of this scene is unmistakable. Fellini is indicating that Guido has projected the anima derived from his mother onto his wife. This, in fact, is the basis for his attraction to her and serves to explain this marriage between people so unlike each other. Luisa, austere, self-righteous, and moralistic, fulfills the same role in Guido's marriage that his mother fulfilled in his childhood. Like his mother, she continually demands that he reform. As Rosella puts it, "What she really wants is for you to be different from what you are."

Thus, when Guido's mother is transformed into his wife
at the end of the cemetery dream, Fellini is explicitly portraying the operation of the anima projection. Another, more
subtle reference can be found in the scene where Guido and
Luisa meet for the first time in front of the village arcade.
They meet in front of a painting of the sea which rests conspicuously in the background as Guido first kisses her.
Throughout the film the sea has been associated with the
anima figure, and here, once again, it seems to suggest that
Luisa fulfills some aspect of his anima projection.

Jung deals explicitly with the manner in which the
mother-imago is transferred to the wife, and views the entire
process in a rather negative light:

> . . . The consequence is that the anima, in the
> form of the mother-imago, is transferred to the wife;
> and the man, as soon as he marries, becomes childish,
> sentimental, dependent, and subservient, or else trucu-
> lent, tyrannical, hypersensitive, always thinking about
> the prestige of his superior masculinity. . . . The
> safeguard against the unconscious, which is what his
> mother meant to him, is not replaced by anything in the
> modern man's education; unconsciously, therefore, his
> ideal of marriage is so arranged that his wife has to
> take over the magical role of the mother. Under the
> cloak of the ideally exclusive marriage he is really
> seeking his mother's protection, and thus he plays into
> the hands of his wife's possessive instincts. . . (Jung,
> Two Essays, p. 208).

Thus, it seems that Guido is victimized by two separate anima
projections.

Guido, of course, rebels against the mother figure. He
seeks qualities which are the polar opposite of those

displayed by the mother. In the Saraghina episode, for instance, these qualities are embodied by Saraghina the whore.
Guido's attraction to Saraghina is his way of rebelling
against the authority of the Church and the hypocritical
morality of his mother. This is particularly clear when he
returns to her in the lyrical conclusion to the episode.
Claudia, the muse, also poses a creative alternative to the
destructive nature of the maternal image. The figure of
Claudia seems to be derived from the women who mothered Guid
as a child, figures, incidentally, who seem far more materna
in the conventional sense than Guido's own mother. As
Guido's most complete anima figure, however, she also shares
attributes of Saraghina as well, which becomes apparent when
she serves as a vehicle for Guido's sexual fantasies in thei
bedroom scene. She embodies all the qualities which Guido
looks for in other women and which he in fact projects upon
them. They are traits which are antithetical in every
respect to the mother-imago.

This seeming opposition between the two anima figures,
one derived from the mother and the other arising from the
rebellion against her, is resolved when it is recognized tha
they are both merely different aspects of the same anima pro
jection. There is an important qualification to be added to
this statement however. The two projections do not exist as
coequals. The mother-imago predominates, and in fact is
always implicit in the nature of the alternative figure the

man is drawn to when he rebels against it. The nature of the
rebellion is conditioned by the attributes one rebels against,
particularly if he is drawn to qualities which are diametric-
ally opposed to them, as is the case when one rebels against
the mother-imago. Thus, the thesis is always implicit in the
antithesis one chooses.

In other words men such as Guido only think they are
attracted to certain women because they view them in terms of
anima projections which are the antithesis of everything that
repelled them in their mothers. In reality, however, they
often choose to cast these misleading projections upon those
women who resemble their mothers the most, and fail to perceive this resemblance, which is the real source of attraction, until it is too late. Thus, the man who is misled by
his anima projections is always doomed to bitter disappoint-
ment.

Ultimately this syndrome results in a kind of emotional
paralysis which prevents the man from ever establishing meaningful relationships with women. Because he views women in
terms which are false and misleading, and ultimately finds
that they remind him of everything he was repelled by in his
mother, he is doomed to continual disillusionment. Often he
will retreat into his dreams where he can fantasize happiness
with women.[10]

[10]Lest this seem too speculative, I draw your attention
to Edward Whitmont's book, The Symbolic Quest, in which he

Throughout the film, Guido experiences this sort of disillusionment. Certainly ample evidence has already been provided of Guido's tendency to retreat into a fantasy world
where he finds gratification by imagining that the women he
knows conform to his every desire. The women upon whom he
has cast his positive anima projection continually disappoint
him by acting instead in the mode of the negative mother-
imago. They are not perfectly submissive; they make demands
upon him. Even Carla, who comes closest perhaps to the ideal
of the totally subservient female, bores Guido by ceaselessly
asking that he give her husband a job. Even she wants him to
love her in return.

His most bitter disillusionment, of course, comes at the
hands of Claudia. In his dreams she most closely epitomizes
the positive anima, the life-giving muse. She fulfills all
his emotional, physical and creative needs while asking
nothing in return. Yet, when she finally appears in person
near the end of the film, she proves to be more reminiscent
of Guido's mother than of his ideal woman. She too makes demands upon him and is critical of the protagonist of his
autobiographical film.

Guido can never see women as they really are. Either
they must be seen in terms of some unattainable ideal, or
else they must be seen as representative of the destructive

describes a case history which conforms to this description
of the double anima in every respect and which seems to be
almost a blueprint of Guido's character in 8-1/2. See
Whitmont, pp. 191-196.

mother-imago. He shifts quickly from one extreme to the other. Either they are entirely on his side or they are entirely in opposition to his interests. He is the prisoner of the two aspects of his anima, and can view women only in terms of these projections. Often they are both equally untrue.

One assumes that Guido was attracted to Luisa as a result of the same psychological process. No doubt he initially viewed her in terms of the subservient anima projection. In terms of their relationship in the film, however, she has clearly come to fulfill the role which his mother once played in his life. The transformation of his mother into Luisa in his dream explicitly points to this.

The harem fantasy supports the contention that as a youth he saw her in far more idealized terms. In the harem fantasy, Luisa plays a very special role. Her position in the harem is quite different from that of the other women. For one thing, she is clearly in charge of the other women at the house, reflecting no doubt her pre-eminence as Guido's wife. Furthermore she does not participate in the rebellion against Guido's authority, but rather stands aloof from it reflecting only admiration for Guido's strength and power and a total look of jealousy.

These are not the only deviations from her usual role. Luisa's entire appearance, in fact, is transformed completely in Guido's fantasy. Throughout the film her appearance has

been austere and rather cold. Both her dress and her general
features are characterized by a sharp, hard, angularity,
rather than by the soft curves traditionally associated with
the supple female. For instance, the angularity of her
sharply chiseled features is underscored by the rectangular
glasses which she wears, and the severe cut of her blouse, as
well as the straight lines of her skirt, serves to augment
and complete the austere and rigid lines which characterize
her appearance. Her short hair, combed absolutely straight,
reinforces this impression and gives her appearance a faintly
masculine quality. In the harem, however, her appearance
changes radically. She wears the simple black dress of the
Italian peasant, and around her waist is wrapped an apron,
signifying her new found domesticity. Her hair is swathed in
a towel, negating the masculine flavor of the short hairdo
she wears in real life. The severe angularity we find in the
appearance of the Luisa who inhabits Guido's real world is no
longer evident. Instead, she exudes warmth and domesticity.
Even the narrow, rectangular glasses have now disappeared.
In every respect she reminds us of the women at the farmhouse
whom Guido remembers from his youth.

All of the harem girls are seen in terms of the anima
projections which first attracted Guido to them. All become
extensions of the women who mothered Guido as a boy, and they
all fulfill this role in the fantasy. Luisa seems to conform
to this role to a far greater degree than do any of the

others. This suggests that Guido's initial attraction to her was also in terms of the submissive anima projection. She occupies the role in the harem that he cast her in when he first loved her. If anything, she embodies the role of the submissive anima figure more completely than any of the other women in the harem, reflecting perhaps the fact that in her case the projection must have been particularly compelling. After all, she is the woman whom he chose to marry, and one usually marries the woman who most fully embodies his anima projection. Ironically, of course, Guido was to find that it was not the submissive anima that Luisa really embodied most completely, but rather the destructive mother-imago. As Whitmont points out, "The anima invariably attracts in terms of its original imprinting" (Whitmont, p. 193).

Yet despite the obvious disillusionment which marriage has represented for Guido, he does not reject Luisa complete-ly, despite his numerous affairs. In fact, she fills a defi-nite need in his life. Guido needs someone to act out the mother-imago role in his life. He seems to have a psychic need for criticism and derision, both because this is the nature of the mother-imago to which he is attracted and be-cause he wants to be punished for the guilt he feels at his sexual adventures. The scorn of his wife is the retribution he desires for the continual sense of guilt he experiences as a result of his Catholic education. He desires her scorn and in fact he elicits it. This is the reason that he invites

Luisa to the spa in the first place. He knows that she will
see Carla, and he wants to be punished in order to compensate
for the guilt which arises from his illicit relationship.

Thus, it is clear that emotionally Guido is at a dead
end. All his relationships with women are doomed to conclude
in hostility. In order to liberate himself from this syndrome, Guido, in Jungian terms, must confront his anima projections and come to understand them. This, indeed, is the
crux of the process of personal development which Jung calls
individuation. On this score, however, the ending of the
film remains profoundly ambiguous, so that the extent to which
Guido has developed along these lines remains in doubt.

II. INDIVIDUATION

Just as the individuation process is a movement towards
psychic wholeness, so 8-1/2 progresses from initial images of
fragmentation, with respect to Guido, to images of wholeness
and unity. We do not even see Guido's face until late in the
second scene, despite the fact that he has been the focal
point of the film's attention from the moment it began.
This, perhaps, is a visual suggestion of Guido's own difficulty in coming to grips with his identity. Moreover, the
shots in the bedroom serve to fragment Guido's body into its
component parts. At first, there are only shots of his hand,
back, and torso, but never his entire body. At one point, he
is lying face down on the bed, with a black cloth, probably

his bathrobe, pulled over the top of his body and draped over
his head. Only his two hands emerge from beneath the cloth,
and he looks rather like a crab. Even when he finally gets
up and walks unsteadily towards the camera his face is bent
downward. Only after he enters the bathroom and looks at
himself in the mirror do we get our first real look at his
face. The fragmentation of Guido's body in this scene is
suggestive of the malaise which grips him throughout most of
the film. His behavior is characterized by confusion and
uncertainty. Unable to cope with middle age, suffering from
a creative blockage, and dominated by his anima projections,
Guido's sense of his own identity seems to be slipping away.

These images of fragmentation at the beginning of the
film contrast sharply with the images of unity at the end.
Many of these latter images are in the Jungian mode. The
dominant motif, for instance, of the final scene is the
circle, a characteristically Jungian emblem of unity. Guido
and all the people he has known form a human chain and dance
around the edge of a huge circus ring. The circle, the
dance, and the human chain are all emblematic of unity in
this context. The visual contrasts between this final scene
and the opening scenes of the film alone suggest that some
fundamental change has occurred in Guido's psyche. More
specifically, the fundamental change in the nature of the
visual content of these scenes suggests that Guido has moved
towards that state of psychic wholeness which denotes

self-realization and is the goal of the individuation
process.

Many critics have attacked the final scene of 8-1/2 as
gratuitous, a happy ending tacked on to the film with no
organic relationship to the wole. According to John Simon
for instance:

> . . . 8-1/2 piles problem upon problem, which is
> permissible; but sheds no light, which is not. There
> is, indeed, a mock resolution tacked on at the end: a
> kind of dance of life begun by a group of clowns which
> includes the hero as boy, and is eventually picked up
> by all the motley dramatis personnae. . . .[11]

This rather popular judgment, however, belies a lack of insight into the true nature of the film. The final scene is
not only appropriate, but in fact it is absolutely necessary.
It serves as an absolutely indispensable conclusion to 8-1/2,
for in this last scene Fellini indicates that Guido begins to
resolve his dilemma, at least in part, by undergoing the
process of individuation. Moreover the images of fragmentation at the beginning of the film are resolved by the images
of unity at the end.

The ambiance of the opening moments of this scene, however, is far less positive. Fellini cuts directly from the
shot of Guido shooting himself in the head to a pan of the
two launching towers. The wind blows fiercely and streamers
billow out from the skeletal towers. The immediate feeling

[11]John Simon, "Fellini's 8-1/2 Fancy," Private
Screenings (New York, 1967), p. 75.

s one of desolation and emptiness. The transition is ambiguous and disorienting. The same wind we hear as Guido shoots
himself blows through this scene. It is not immediately
clear that the film has returned to the real world.

The camera, panning to the left, finally rests upon a
view of the top of the second tower which is identical to the
view of it we see in the opening nightmare as Guido flies
through the clouds. This tends to give that earlier shot the
aspect of a flash forward. Since this view of the tower is a
visual reference to Saraghina it suggests that the anima
principle will play a crucial role in the scene. In fact, it
soon becomes apparent that the focal point of the climactic
fantasy is Guido's women.

First, we see a close-up of Claudia smiling. She turns
to the left, and in a long shot walks off screen toward the
left, a reversal of the direction in which she moves when she
first appears at the garden of the spa. Significantly, we
are never to see her again.

This shot is followed by a close-up of Carla, dressed
completely in white, walking towards the right. In the background other figures from Guido's life, such as the Cardinal,
can also be seen walking towards the right. The opposition
between the direction of their movements and that of Claudia's
is immediately apparent. All are dressed in white. This
shot is followed by another in which entire groups of people
drawn from Guido's past, all dressed in white, are seen

walking towards the right.

Guido strokes his hair, and we hear his thoughts upon the sound track as he experiences the sudden burst of insight which structures the final scene. "What is this sudden joy?" he asks. The film cuts to a shot of Luisa and Rosella walking slowly towards the camera in a circus ring. Both of the women are dressed in white. As Guido's internal monologue continues, we hear him ask, for the first time in the movie, for forgiveness. "Forgive me, sweet creatures," he says, "I didn't understand. I didn't know." As Guido begins to speak, Luisa continues to walk towards the camera, but Rosella pauses and stays behind. "I do accept you. I do love you . . . ," Guido continues, "How simple it is." Luisa now has moved to close-up range. Behind her we can see Rosella in the background. She walks off to the left, her hands in her pockets. Like Claudia, she never returns. For the first time in the film, and perhaps in Guido's life, he has honestly expressed his love for somebody, even if only in fantasy. Having run out of excuses and evasions, he accepts the validity of Claudia's implicit criticism, that he does not know how to love, and begins to change. "Luisa," he says, "I've been freed."

This, then, is the moment of epiphany in 8-1/2. In a sudden burst of insight, which he calls "this sudden joy," Guido comes to understand that he must extend as well as receive love. At the same time he is "freed," both from the

emotional paralysis which cripples every aspect of his life
and the domination of the anima projections which have alienated him from the world. In fact, his liberation from the
anima's dominance is explicitly rendered in the image of
Claudia leaving him at the beginning of the fantasy. She
walks off to the left, while all the other figures in the
scene walk towards the right.[12] Claudia has no place in the
final circle, because the anima projection, pleasant though
it might be, has served to alienate Guido from his world and
those around him. Her departure is the first sign that Guido
will no longer view the world in terms of his false and misleading projections. The theme of the final scene is thus
one of reconciliation and acceptance. Guido appears ready to
accept and love people in his life as they are, rather than
in terms of any false ideal. Thus, he says to Luisa, "I do
accept you."

Rosella also walks off screen forever at this moment.
Like Claudia she walks off toward the left, leaving the circus ring before the others arrive. Throughout the film she
has served as a kind of mediator between Guido and Luisa,
telling Guido, for instance, what he must do to please his

[12]Suzanne Budgen makes much the same point when she
says, ". . . The magician says that everything is now ready,
and beckons to the Ideal, who smiles at Guido, sustaining him
for his final effort. Later, when Guido has embraced his new
life, she walks away, not directly away from the camera, but
across the screen in the opposite direction from that taken,
in other shots, by all the others. She has no part in the
final circle" (Budgen, p. 64).

wife. In his fantasy Guido is saying that they will no
longer need anybody to play this role for them, that they
will be able to deal with each other directly without inter-
mediaries to interpret their wishes.

Finally, Guido says, "The truth is . . . I do not know,
I seek . . . I have not yet found. Only with this in mind
can I feel alive and look at you without shame. Life is a
holiday. Let us live it together." Luisa remains expression
less. He continues, "That is all I can say, Luisa, to you
and the others. Accept me as I am. Only then will we discover each other."

This passage is crucial. Having expressed his acceptanc
of Luisa, Guido now asks her to accept him as he is, with all
his failings. He is not promising to be faithful. Later, in
fact, the other women in his life join in the final dance.
Therefore, he asks Luisa to accept him along with his philan-
dering, and not to judge him against an anachronistic standard of marital fidelity to which he is unable to adhere.[13]

At this point, the ambiguity of the scene becomes quite
evident. Guido, despite his new insight into the need to

---

[13]Angelo Solmi, in his book Fellini, suggests that
acceptance is one of the major themes of 8-1/2 and cites
Fellini to back up his contention, "'What I should like most,
Fellini confesses even today, 'is that 8-1/2 should banish
the neurotic complexes that obsess people who want to change
others. I think people should be taken as they are. If the
film restored this sense of freedom, then it succeeded. So
8-1/2 is a film of liberation--nothing more. . . .'" Angelo
Solmi, Fellini, trans. by Elizabeth Greenwood (London, 1967),
p. 171.

love others seems as detached from reality as ever.

Guido says that he accepts Luisa and asks her to accept him as he is. She responds, "I'm not sure that's true, but I can try if you'll help me." In imagining this response, Guido negates the validity of his prior statement. He has said that he accepts her, presumably as she is, and then imagines her responding to his request in a manner that is completely out of character. Luisa, as we have seen her in the film, is clearly incapable of such a response, for her behavior has been characterized all along by her inability to acquiesce in Guido's unfaithfulness and his lies. Yet, if she is to accept him as he is, which is what he asks, she must presumably accept him as a man who will continue to betray her and, even worse, lie to her about it. For Guido to assume that she will now accept such an arrangement just because he declares that he loves her is not really to accept her as she is, but rather to imagine that she has fundamentally changed. Thus, the entire scene seems hollow, pathetic, and self-serving. It is Luisa who must make all the concessions. In this respect, the concluding fantasy of the film is no different from all the others. Guido's recognition of the need to love, while an advance, represents something less than a total psychic revolution.

Thus, the final scene takes on a rather ambiguous quality, for it encompasses two themes which contradict each other. On one hand, the dominant motif of the final scene

is one of unity. He seems to transcend barriers which had
formerly alienated him from the world. At the same time,
however, he assumes that the past can be revoked in one fell
swoop, that, for instance, Luisa, with little protest, will
overlook everything that has come between them over the last
twenty years. In the conversation just related, then, Luisa
is depicted as falsely as she is in the harem fantasy.
Guido's individuation then, at the end of the film, does not
necessarily put him in touch with the real world. New lies
replace the old.

A few critics, in fact, have commented upon the unsatis-
factory nature of Guido's conversion at the end of the film.
Dwight McDonald, for instance, says that:

> . . . I didn't for a minute believe that Guido had
> changed: the reconciliation with his wife . . . was un-
> integrated fantasy, as was the affectionate kiss he
> gives his mistress. On the plane of real behavior, his
> wife will continue to be censorious, his mistress will
> continue to be vulgar, and he will continue to betray
> both of them and will greedily try to get love without
> giving love.[14]

Similarly, Armando Favazza objects that, "He has not con-
quered his parasite; he has simply gained the momentary upper
hand by achieving an insight about which we are not told."[15]
These writers do not find Guido's conversion to be very con-
vincing, but they do not deal with the dichotomy which lies

[14]McDonald, p. 22.

[15]Amando Favazza, "Fellini: Analyst without Portfolio,"
Man and the Movies (Baltimore, 1967), p. 185.

t the root of the ambiguity which pervades the scene, namely
he opposition between his individuation, on the one hand,
nd his negation of time, on the other. In the former case
e moves towards an acceptance of reality, while in the later he attempts to deny it in a new way. Finally, it is the
ame old Guido. He still dreams that the woman will be sub-
ervient to his desires.

The primary emphasis of the final scene does seem to be
n unity and reconciliation, in keeping with the theme of
individuation. The major visual motif representative of this
heme of unity is that of the circle, in this case the circus
ring. It is an image derived directly from Jung. Aniela
Jaffe describes, for instance, the circle as the major archetypal representation of psychic unity:

> Dr. M.-L. von Franz has explained the circle (or
> sphere) as a symbol of the Self. It expresses the
> totality of the psyche in all its aspects, including the
> relationship between man and the whole of nature.[16]

The circle, for Jung, is a type of mandala, an archetypal symbol which recurs in all cultures as a representation
of the total self. In fact, according to the glossary of
Memories, Dreams, Symbols, the Hindu word "mandala" means
magic circle:

> Mandala (Sanskrit). Magic Circle. In Jung, symbol of
> the center, the goal, or the self (q.v.) as psychic
> totality; self-representation of a psychic process of

[16]Aniela Jaffe, "Symbolism in the Visual Arts," Man and
His Symbols (New York, 1964), p. 266.

centering; production of a new center pf personality.
This is symbolically represented by the circle, the
square, or the quaternity (q.v.), by symmetrical arrange-
ments of the number four and its multiples. . . .[17]

Most mandalas incorporate the four-fold structure Jung calls

the quaternity. Often they consist of squares, circles with-

in squares, squares within circles, or circles divided into

four equal parts. Even the cross can be viewed as a mandala.

The circle alone, however, is a sufficient representation of

the archetype, and, as we have seen, its name is synonymous

with circle.

The fact that the circle-as-mandala is an archetype of

psychic unity alone would make it an apt visual motif with

which to conclude the film, for Guido, in integrating his

anima projections heals the schism in his psyche. The arche-

type, however, is also associated with the spirit of recon-

ciliation which is so basic to the conclusion of 8-1/2.[18]

The archetypal significance of the circus ring which domi-

nates the finale of 8-1/2 by now is evident. The circus ring

is an archetype representative of the new sense of psychic

[17]C. G. Jung, Memories, Dreams, Symbols, trans. by
Richard and Clara Winston (New York, 1961), p. 396. Subsequent references included in the text as Jung, Memories.

[18]As Jung puts it in Flying Saucers: ". . . They [the
UFO's] are impressive manifestations of totality whose simple,
round form portrays the archetype of self, which as we know
from experience plays the chief role in uniting apparently
irreconciliable opposites and is therefore best suited to
compensate for the split-mindedness of our age. . . ." C. G.
Jung, Flying Saucers, trans. R. F. C. Hull (New York, 1969),
p. 32.

wholeness which follows the integration of the anima projections.

One more detail reinforcing the archetypal significance
of the circle deserves mention. After Luisa promises to try
to accept Guido, a band of clowns, reminiscent of those in La
Strada, marches across the screen followed by Guido as a
schoolboy. Now the school uniform is white. In view of the
significance Jung attaches to the quaternity as an aspect of
the mandala, perhaps it should also be mentioned that there
are four clowns.

After confronting Luisa, Guido enters the circus ring and
begins to direct the activities of the people within. In
other words, he imagines himself directing the fantasy much
as he would direct a movie. He points the band toward their
places and whispers directions in the boy's ear. Then,
speaking through a bullhorn, he begins to direct the other
people in the ring.

The boy, playing his flute, leaves the band of clowns
and walks to the right of a huge curtain. The music swells
as the curtain opens revealing the staircase which leads up
the launching tower. A mass of people, in fact all the
people Guido has ever known, begin descending the stairs toward the camera, in a shot which is the reversal of the one
in which the producer led his entourage up the tower at night
earlier in the film. These are people of secondary importance in Guido's life, unlike the people seen walking towards

the circle earlier, and, therefore, unlike them they are not dressed entirely in white. As the crowd begins to stream past the camera, one sees familiar faces, Guido's producer, Conocchia, and Daumier. Guido, bullhorn in hand, directs them towards their places on the rim of the circus ring.

Carla then joins Guido in the center of the ring. Immediately it is clear that Guido has no thought of relinquishing his former lifestyle. "I understand," says Carla, "you're to say you can't do without us. Will you call me tomorrow?" Guido pinches her cheek affectionately and answers, "Yes, but now go join the others."

Then as the dance begins, Guido rejoins Luisa and takes her hand, but she pauses for a moment, looks over her shoulder, and seems hesitant to follow his lead. Then she relents and follows him as they walk towards the dancers in the background. Luisa mounts the rim and joins the chain dance followed by Guido. They become part of the circle.

The emphasis upon unity and reconciliation in the scene is rather obvious. The reconciliation is not merely between Guido and his wife. It extends to all the people he knows or has ever known. They all dance together in chain. The dance itself, in fact, is one of the key motifs underscoring the theme of unity in this scene. The fact that Guido and his friends dance upon the rim of the circus ring enhances the impact of the circle as an archetype of unity and reconciliation.

In fact, dancing is a predominant motif throughout the film, and is always associated with unity and reconcilia-tion.[19] One recalls the scene of old couples dancing at the spa's night club and particularly Mezzabotta's valiant attempts to keep up with Gloria's energetic dancing as a kind of justification of their relationship. In the harem the black girl dances Saraghina's rhumba in order to prove her-self worthy of membership in the harem. Dancing is a test of membership in the harem, later failed by Jacqueline, and this underscores the fact that the harem is the place where all Guido's women are reconciled. Moreover, Guido and Luisa dance when they meet. Luisa and Carla dance when they become friends in Guido's fantasy.

The final scene is the culmination of this motif. Here everyone in the film dances hand in hand in a circle of unity. The reconciliation between Guido and his wife is just the most important aspect of a general reconciliation of all the divergent characters who inhabit Guido's world. Guido dances with Luisa, she dances with all Guido's other women, and even the Cardinal dances with Saraghina. Since the en-tire scene arises in Guido's imagination, we can also assume that it represents the integration of all the divergent as-pects of his psyche, such as the mother and the muse or the saint and the whore, which is, after all, the ultimate goal

[19]For another discussion of the dancing motif in 8-1/2, see Ted Perry, "Signifiers."

of the individuation process.

Throughout the entire film, Fellini has consistently emphasized Guido's isolation from the others in his world. Here, at the end of the film, Guido breaks through the barriers of solitude which have separated him from others throughout the film, and becomes one with the world around him. Whereas earlier the camera work had served to isolate him from them, he now becomes an indistinguishable part of the entire chain of humanity.[20]

Yet, despite this emphasis on reconciliation the scene remains ambiguous. Although the individuation process is supposed to put the subject more directly in touch with reality, there are many elements in the episode which suggest that Guido has yet to honestly face the reality of his condition. For instance, the easy comradery of the dancers

[20]Ted Perry has pointed out how Fellini's camera work serves to isolate Guido from his environment. After Guido enters the circus ring at the end of the film, however, the final scene is shot almost exclusively in long shots which serve to establish his relationship with his environment. As Suzanne Budgen puts it, ". . . The last sequence, in other words, contains and reconciles all the separate elements in the film, showing forth the integration in Guido of everything that has been dividing him. Only in this one sequence is he wholly present in body, mind, and spirit, for in the one other sequence where his mind seems to be on what he is doing, namely the interview with the Cardinal, his body is not there. We see and hear the Cardinal and his attendants, but we do not see Guido at all" (Budgen, p. 65). Only in the concluding fantasy does the camera cease to separate Guido from his environment and, instead, establish and reinforce his relationship to it. At the end, when he becomes an indistinguishable part of the chain dance, of course, he blends with it completely.

minds us of nothing so much as the friendship of the women
Guido's harem. Luisa's promise to try to accept Guido,
though given reluctantly, conforms so perfectly to Guido's
pes and desires that it seems completely out of character.
e seems uncharacteristically humble and submissive, promis-
g to try to accept him if he will help her. The only time
have seen Luisa act like this before is at the end of the
rem episode when, on her hands and knees scrubbing the
oor, she literally prostrates herself before Guido. So
re too, Guido's fantasy seems to be at odds with what we
ow about the people in Guido's world.

One might argue at this point that, after all, the scene
 a fantasy, and that one does not hold fantasies to scrupu-
us standards of verisimilitude. This concluding fantasy,
owever, seems to be structured, at least in part, upon the
remise that Guido through his imagination, is beginning to
ome to grips with his world; it presupposes that Guido has
ome to recognize certain truths which put him in touch more
irectly with reality.

Yet the reconciliation with Luisa suggests a lingering
nability to face the truth directly and unflinchingly. Not
nly is the scene as self-serving as any of Guido's earlier
antasies, but also it denies the reality of time by suggest-
ng that the past can be revoked or, more precisely, that it
an be restructured. Inherent in the fantasy is the assump-
ion that unpleasant memories of the past can instantaneously

be dismissed by one act of good will. Guido believes that
you can go home again, that empty and bitter relationships
can be renewed as if the bitterness had never arisen. Thus,
Luisa, with little real objection, agrees to try to accept
Guido as he is, presumably including his lying and philander-
ing. He, on the other hand, does not really accept her as
she is, but rather imagines her acting completely out of
character. It is as if he turns the clock back twenty years,
wiping out all the unpleasant associations with the past and
beginning the marriage anew. Similarly, all the people in
Guido's life reunite as if nothing had ever come between
them. Thus, the concluding fantasy is escapist in the sense
that Guido envisions the world as it might exist if everyone
would just forget the past and accept each other on altogether new premises.

This desire to turn the clock back and obliterate the
past finds its visual expression in the fact that Guido's
friends dance counter-clockwise about the circus ring. This
movement is conspicuous in the scene. At first, as the first
few people gather on the rim, they begin to dance tentatively
in a clockwise direction. They seem unsure of themselves and
soon they halt marking time on the rim. Clockwise is the
wrong direction. Later, when Guido gives the proper signal,
Maurice leads them counter-clockwise around the circle.
Their reconciliation is a denial of the corrosive effects of
time. In Guido's fantasy, one act of love negates all the

bitterness and strife that had gone before.

This longing to begin anew is expressed in other ways as
well. All of the major figures from Guido's past, the ones
who enter from the beach, are wearing white. Previously,
only Claudia has been associated with the color white in
Guido's fantasies. In the person of Claudia, the color white
is explicitly associated with purity and simplicity, qualities Guido draws from his past. They are the qualities which
Guido longs for in the past. Thus, when the significant figures from Guido's past reappear in white at the end of the
film, he is clearly viewing them in terms of these same vir-
tues. Once more, therefore, Fellini visually depicts Guido's
desire to turn back the clock and return to a state of purity
and innocence which he associates with the past. Guido sup-
poses that the memory of events which served to alienate
these people from him and from each other can be obliterated
in one fell swoop and that they can join together in a new
sense of universal love. This is the sense of purity and
innocence represented for him by the color white in this
scene. It is the purity which stems from obliterating the
past, and of returning to a state in which it does not count.

The return of Guido as a boy can be seen in the same
light. He is held by the nurses as a young boy and he
marches in his school uniform as a somewhat older boy. It
too is white. The boy represents something very essential in
Guido. As Suzanne Budgen puts it, "The child Guido holds the

key to everything that figures in the experience of the man
(Budgen, p. 65). Everything that Guido does in the film is
conditioned by his childhood. But here the child represents
as well, a lost innocence that can never really be regained

When all the people he has known appear in white at the
end of the film, the effect is strikingly unreal. It is
startling to see Saraghina, for instance, the epitome of sin
fulness, dressed in pristine white. The total effect is to
suggest that Guido is only deluding himself once more. It i
a delusion to think that innocence can ever be regained. It
is a delusion to think that one can ever begin with a clean
slate again.

Thus, the film is finally ambiguous. Guido does learn
how to love, he does transcend his alienation, and he does
regain his creative power. But time seems to have run out o
him. His life lies about him in ruins. He has vacillated t
long, and his dream that he can somehow turn the clock back
and pick up the pieces seems empty and futile.

Fellini sees the final ambiguity of the film in a more
positive light. He suggests that in the film everyone is
vindicated:

> . . . But I maintain that it is a positive work,
> more positive than La Dolce Vita, and that it has no
> negative characters. Take the critic who consistently
> and bitterly derides Guido's efforts to escape from the
> moral abyss into which he has fallen (and at one point
> Guido sees him hanged, in his daydream). Well, even he
> is a positive character, because he is right to quarrel
> with the hero. In fact, everyone in the film is right,

Guido with his faults, his wife, the priests in their
seminary who say that Saraghina is the devil (and to a
certain extent she does represent the devil), and even
Saraghina herself (Solmi, p. 171).

No doubt this sense of universal vindication underlies the
pattern of reconciliation at the end of the film. All the
characters accept each other as they are. Guido accepts
Luisa and she accepts him. But even this sense of reconciliation seems finally empty. All this means is that nothing
finally has changed. As Dwight McDonald suggests, Guido will
continue to betray Luisa and she will continue to scorn him.
The only thing that will have changed is that now they will
accept the hopelessness of escaping the game they are condemned to play out till the end.

The ending of the film is thus complex and ambiguous on
every level. Even though, on the psychological level, the
individuation process is fulfilled, this does not mean that
Guido has by any means resolved his problems completely.
While he confronts reality in one sphere and integrates the
anima figure within his total personality, he continues to
evade it on another by denying the reality of time.

This kind of psychological depth is just one major
aspect of a first-person point of view which pervades and
structures the entire film. This paper began with a demonstration of how the visual aspects of 8-1/2, even in scenes
situated in the real world, were structured upon the first-
person point of view. It then examined the extension of the
first-person point of view into Guido's fantasies, dreams and

memories, some of which occasionally intrude upon the real
world. Finally it demonstrated that the relationship betwee
reality and fantasy in the film reflects the in-depth psycho
logical operations of the mind which dominates the film.
Perhaps no other film in the history of the cinema has succeeded so completely in representing directly on the screen
the operation of a single human intelligence at every psycho
logical level. This, no doubt, is 8-1/2's most significant
contribution to the art of the cinema.

CHAPTER IV

THE AUTOBIOGRAPHICAL FALLACY

It has become commonplace in film criticism to assume that 8-1/2, because it deals with the problems of a film director, is primarily an autobiographical work. Many critics, either explicitly or implicitly, equate Guido with Fellini. Suzanne Budgen, for instance, reasons as follows:

> Fellini is the most egotistic of film-makers and the most autobiographical, and on the face of it 8-1/2 is only the logical outcome of this normal method, a Fellini film raised to the nth power, an open declaration that this, once and for all, is a complete self-revelation. And yet in a sense 8-1/2 is the least private of all of his films. It is not so much a revelation of himself as an exposition of his persona. It is the interview to end all interviews. Here Fellini is telling us in his own person--Guido is a carefully deliberate self-portrait--things which in earlier films had been revealed to us obliquely, and at first sight it may seem that he is not greatly adding to what we know already. . . . And yet, when the physical presence of the film is familiar to us, we gradually discover layer upon layer of private richness put before us under the cover of the explicit self-portrait. . . (Budgen, p. 57).

John Simon, in attacking the film, makes much the same point in a different context:

> Now comes 8-1/2 and despite two or three good scenes, it is a disheartening fiasco. There are several reasons for this. First, it is extremely hard, virtually impossible, to make a good autobiography out of one's present. The present hurts too much. . . (Simon, p. 74).

Not only does Dwight McDonald see the film as Fellini's
autobiography, but he also extrapolates beyond this point to
assert that the film which Guido decides to make at the end
of 8-1/2 is identical to it:

> . . . Guido gets out of the car, takes up his
> director's bullhorn and begins to arrange everybody; he
> has decided to make an entirely different movie, about
> himself--his memories, his women, his creative prob-
> lems--in short, the movie we have just seen. . .
> (McDonald, p. 21).

Suzanne Budgen echoes the same line of reasoning when she
says, with reference to the screen test episode, that:

> . . . Since the screen tests turn out to be for the
> very film that we are watching, of which these screen
> tests are a part, we are seized, temporarily, with a
> bewilderment equal to Luisa's own. It is a brilliant
> feat (Budgen, pp. 59-60).

Both of these writers, as well as others, see 8-1/2 as
ultimately being a reflexive work of art, a film within a
film. The most comprehensive and elaborate interpretation of
the film in this light occurs in "La construction 'en abyme'
dans Huit et Demi, de Fellini" by Christian Metz. He com-
pares the structure of the film to the "construction en
abyme," a heraldic device resembling the effect of a series
of successive reflections in a series of mirrors, in which
the design of the device is perfectly reproduced in ever
diminishing size so that it seems to recede within itself.
In this respect, he argues that 8-1/2 is unique, for while a
significant number of films depict other films being planned
or made, 8-1/2 is the only one in which the film we see is

identical to the one the protagonist dreams of making.[1]
Thus, strangely enough, because Guido appears in the film he
dreams of making, he begins to merge with Fellini.

Metz's proposal that 8-1/2 is identical with the film
within the film is certainly a clever and attractive idea,
and one which other critics have tacitly suggested. Yet, the
idea does not bear up under careful scrutiny. It is not at
all certain, for instance, that the evidence, once examined
(a process French critics seem reluctant to engage in), supports Metz's contention that the film which Guido dreams of
making is, in fact, 8-1/2. Surely it is true that many of
Guido's fantasies are projections of scenes which he intends
to include in his film and has already included in his script.
For instance, while on their way to meet the Cardinal in the
garden of the spa, the lay associate criticizes Guido's plan
to depict the hero of his film meeting the Cardinal in the
baths. Later, when in the steam room, Guido fantasizes a
meeting between himself and the Cardinal as the Cardinal takes
a mud bath. Similarly, at the end of the Saraghina episode,
we find Guido and Daumier eating lunch while the critic
attacks the scene we have just witnessed as being too sentimental for the script. The scene arises in Guido's memory,
is included in his script, and appears in 8-1/2, and

---

[1]Christian Metz, "La construction 'en abyme' dans Huit
et Demi, de Fellini," Essais sur la Signification au Cinéma
(Paris, 1968), pp. 224-226.

Daumier's attack can be viewed ironically as an attack upon 8-1/2 as well as upon Guido's script, since at this point they do coincide. Fellini, in fact, is parodying his critics before they attack. But is this evidence sufficient to suggest that in every respect the film which Guido wants to make is 8-1/2? We might view Daumier's notes attacking the appearance of Claudia at the fountain in Guido's film which the director reads immediately after the same vision has just occurred in 8-1/2 in much the same light and ask just the same question. Similarly, the fact that he screen tests women to play the parts of the chief women in his life does not necessarily mean that he intends to make the film which turns out to be 8-1/2.

In fact, several possibilities for the film Guido intends to make are suggested throughout 8-1/2. First of all, there is the space epic for which the rocket launching platform has been built. The world is destroyed by a nuclear holocaust and the survivors, the Catholic clergy in the lead, flee aboard rocket ships. Certainly this film bears little resemblance to 8-1/2. To be fair, it does seem as if he has abandoned this scheme in favor of a more autobiographical work but has not yet found courage to tell the producer. Other than the launching pads, there is little evidence that he still plans to make this film, while the erection of the towers does provide him with the means of buying time. On the other hand, since he tells Rosella that his film will

include everything and everybody, perhaps we are to assume
that somehow he is still attempting to salvage his old plan
for a space epic by restructuring it in terms of his autobiography. His own confusion, however, makes any affirmative
assertion in this regard rather difficult.

When he first envisions Claudia in his room, he speculates as to what kind of role she could play in his film. He
speculates that there could be a museum in the village and
that she could be the curator's daughter. "You've grown up
surrounded by classical art and beauty," he says. Ironically
the camera deflates his romanticism by focusing upon the bed
strewn with cheesecake photographs, a point which is underscored by the fact that as the camera pans upward to Claudia
reading the script she bursts into laughter. It is not
clear, of course, whether Guido is attempting to work her
into his space epic or whether he is contriving a new film
about her. The only thing that is clear is that he is not
thinking in terms of the film we know as 8-1/2.

Finally, there is, of course, the autobiographical film
he has decided to make, perhaps in lieu of the space epic.
This is the film which Metz refers to as the film within a
film which is the film itself. He identifies it with 8-1/2.
Guido has decided to make a film about his life so that, like
David Holzman, he can analyze and understand it. He fails,
of course, because he does not understand that he must come
to grips with his life before he can convert it into art.

The process does not operate in reverse. If he does not come
to terms with his existence he can scarcely expect to be able
to transform it into a work of art.

At any rate, Metz identifies this autobiographical film
with 8-1/2, and it is certainly true that many of the scenes
to be included in it appear directly in 8-1/2 in the form of
Guido's fantasies and memories. The appearance of Claudia at
the spa, the Saraghina episode, and the audience with the
Cardinal in the baths are all part of Guido's film as well as
of 8-1/2. At the end of the film, Guido tells Claudia the
actress that she will play the part of a girl at the springs,
which suggests both that the girl in white whose presence
Guido hallucinates will become an actual person in his film
and that the film itself will take place at the springs which
serve as the setting for 8-1/2. Finally, the screen tests
for Guido's film are presented directly in 8-1/2, and we
learn that all of the important women in his life are to be
portrayed in his film. Clearly then, 8-1/2 does often coincide with his projected work. At no point, however, is it
ever suggested that Guido's film will be identical to the one
which we experience as 8-1/2, and, in fact, as we have seen,
Guido seems to have many different plans in mind for his film
among which he is unable to make a definitive choice.

Furthermore, to suggest that Guido's film is identical
to 8-1/2 is to imply that somehow Guido is identical to
Fellini, that in some sense he is the author of 8-1/2. Metz

himself implies this, although he demurs that the resemblance
between the two is only general. Others are more positive.
Dwight McDonald suggests, as we have seen, that at the end of
the film Guido goes off to make 8-1/2. Along with other
critics, he is suggesting that not only is Guido's film autobiographical but also that Fellini's is as well. The reflexive nature of the film is deepened, for 8-1/2 thus becomes
the autobiography of both Guido and Fellini. It is the autobiographical film which Guido planned to make as well as the
autobiography of Fellini. In the process Guido merges with
Fellini and becomes an autobiographical projection of him.
Ultimately, this is the implication of even Metz's argument
even though he maintains that the resemblance between the two
is only general. When he says that 8-1/2 is the film which
Guido dreams of making, that the film within the film is
identical to the film itself, one has little choice but to
conclude that Guido is Fellini. Any other conclusion reduces
Metz's argument to mere gibberish, suggesting that a totally
fictional character is the author of the work in which he
appears.

Let us then examine Metz's only way out of this dilemma.
Assuredly, Fellini himself has confessed that 8-1/2 has an
autobiographical flavor. Angelo Solmi, for instance, quotes
Fellini in the following terms:

> 'I realize that 8-1/2 is such a shameless and
> brazen confession,' Fellini said to me, 'that it is
> futile to try and make people forget that it is about

my own life. But I try to make a film that pleases me, first of all, and then the public. In 8-1/2 the boundary line between what I did for myself and what I created for the public is very subtle' (Solmi, p. 171).

Furthermore, there is ample evidence to suggest that many of the incidents which occur in 8-1/2 are drawn from Fellini's own life. Deena Boyer, for instance, relates how the Saraghina episode is drawn from Fellini's own past (Boyer, pp. 173-174). Furthermore, many other details from Guido's past also coincide with Fellini's, such as the harsh Jesuit education.

Moreover, incidents which occurred during the making of the film are incorporated within it. When Guido greets his producer in the hotel lobby, for instance, the producer tells him that the Americans have just signed. L'Avant Scène points out that this line was drawn directly from Fellini's own experience in making 8-1/2. When Fellini's producer, Rizzoli, ran short of money he decided to show some footage to American distributors. Fellini quickly concluded the harem scene and this episode was shown to them. They signed immediately for the distribution rights in America.[2] Dwight McDonald also says that Joseph E. Levine handed out $140,000 just to build the rocket launching tower (McDonald, p. 17).

Guido clearly shares a few of Fellini's more famous directorial quirks. He casts largely by faces, as does

[2]Federico Fellini, "8-1/2," L'Avant-Scène du Cinéma, No. 63, p. 22.

ellini. He rejects the old men for the part of his father

ecause they do not look old enough. Like Fellini, Guido

pends extravagantly upon his films. Like Fellini, who often

rites his dialogue for a scene just before it is shot, Guido

athers all the resources for his film about him and then

elies on inspiration to provide him with a script. In this

egard, Fellini encountered difficulties in making 8-1/2 sim-

lar to those Guido faced in making his film. Angelo Solmi

oints out the similarities between Guido and Fellini in this

egard in the following passage:

> 'When I said that I didn't even know what the plot
> was,' Fellini declared, 'journalists thought I was telling
> one of my habitual lies. Instead for me it was the
> truth. I was looking for the Juno-like woman, I was
> busy, I appeared to have it all worked out in my head,
> but it was not like that. For three months I continued
> working on the basis of a complete production, in the
> hope that meanwhile my ideas would sort themselves out.
> Fifty times I was on the point of taking Francassi, the
> production director, by the arm and saying, "I can't
> remember the story any more, I can't go on making it."
> In short, the preparation was torture. Afterwards
> everything was easy.'
> 'And no one suspected anything?'
> 'They had faith in me, they thought I knew what I
> was doing, that keeping the plot a secret from the
> actors was a great publicity stunt. In fact, all this
> became the film itself, or rather gave it unity. Two
> days before filming I was about to go to the producer and
> tell him the truth outright, begging him to stop the
> machinery of organization. But how do you tell a man of
> integrity: "I can't make a film that I can't remember,
> please excuse me, it was all a joke." Even he wouldn't
> have believed me' (Solmi, pp. 167-168).

Although most of Fellini's doubts, like Guido's, had

been in the preparatory stages of the film, Solmi describes

how they were rumored to have existed throughout the entire

shooting of the film (Solmi, p. 167). The film was shot in
an atmosphere of mystery. Nobody knew the entire plot of the
film, not even the leading actors. Solmi describes persist-
ent rumors that Fellini could not finish the film. Fellini
himself liked to call the film his "Unfinished." Because of
the erection of the space towers, it was rumored that
Fellini, like Guido, was making a science-fiction film.

Solmi's description of the making of 8-1/2 is substanti-
ated in Deena Boyer's book, The Two Hundred Days of 8-1/2.
Her account of the making of the film is rife with mystery
and confusion. Although she worked on the film as an "on-set
press officer," she knew only the barest essentials about the
plot. The scenario was merely a skeletal outline of the
film, and often Fellini feverishly typed the dialogue on the
set minutes before it was used (Boyer, p. 128; p. 198). Most
of the actors, with the exception of Mastroianni, had little
idea of the true nature of their parts, and the fact that
they often got their dialogue only a half-hour before shooting prevented them from developing interpretations of the
characters which diverged from Fellini's own desires.

Although she records constant delays in the start of
production, Miss Boyer is apparently unaware of the fundamental uncertainties which Solmi reports as having plagued
Fellini even before the film was made. She does, however,
report in some detail his difficulties in deciding upon an
ending for the film. The first ending shot took place in a

railroad car, but Fellini was evidently unsatisfied with it
from the start. Later he shot the dance of reconciliation
which now concludes the film. Almost everyone connected with
the production seemed unaware of what he was doing, and most
seemed to have assumed that the dance would be the opening
sequence of the film (Boyer, pp. 183-192). Later Boyer
records the struggle which took place in Fellini's own mind
before he definitely decided to end the film with the dance
sequence.

Thus, it is clear that Fellini was wracked with indeci-
sion, particularly in the pre-production phases of the film,
in much the same way that Guido is in 8-1/2. The difference,
of course, is that while Fellini might have been indecisive,
Guido is blocked.[3]

This last distinction is crucial to a resolution of the
question of the reflexiveness of the film. Despite all the
similarities between Guido and Fellini one must finally conclude that, in the last analysis, they are not identical. In
no sense can Guido be equated with Fellini, despite the
attempts of numerous critics to do so. While there are certainly autobiographical elements in 8-1/2, the film is not

---

[3]A curious footnote to all of this is that, following
Juliet of the Spirits, Fellini embarked upon the production
of a film called The Voyage of G. Mastorna, listed as an im-
miediate project on page 92 of L'Avant-Scène, which was never
made. A number of sets which had already been constructed by
the filmmaker were later abandoned when the film failed to
materialize.

Fellini's autobiography. Like many creative artists, Fellin
draws upon his own experiences during the creative process,
and often these experiences emerge in some form in his work.
But it is rather naive to conclude from this evidence that
the protagonist of the work is identical to the author.
Critics who fail even to make this most elementary of dis-
tinctions perhaps should be in another line of work. Fellin
has often been compared to Joyce, particularly in terms of
8-1/2, but it would be no more valid to suggest that Fellini
is Guido than it is to suggest that Joyce is Daedelus. Both
characters share attributes of their authors, but in both
cases the proper aesthetic distance, a factor Joyce insisted
upon, is maintained. Neither character can or should be con
fused with his author. This was a point which Joyce insiste
upon, and which Fellini emphasizes as well.

Beyond the obvious point that many of the conditions an
circumstances of Guido's life, such as his relationship with
his wife and his bitter introversion, are totally unlike
Fellini's, Fellini himself, as described by Peter Harcourt,
is adamant in emphasizing the differences between himself an
Guido, and in debunking the notion that somehow Guido can be
considered the author of 8-1/2. In fact, Fellini suggests
that one of the crucial differences between Guido and himsel
is that Guido failed to make his film while Fellini complete
his:

Beneath the astonishing technical virtuousity of the film . . . there is an inner argument at its center that has a surprising toughness about it, that shows itself as being very critical of the attitude adopted by Guido Anselmi who we have a right to imagine bears a strong resemblance to Fellini himself; except--as Fellini himself has been quick to point out--Guido was unable to finish his film while Fellini achieved <u>8-1/2</u>.[4]

To suggest that Guido is the author of <u>8-1/2</u> is to miss completely the poignant quality of the film's ending. Guido's revelation is too late. The set is being struck. He imagines his producer telling him that he will never work again, and there is certainly considerable truth in this fantasy. He has overcome his creative block, but his time has run out. Similarly, although he learns to love his wife, she has already walked out of his life.

Throughout the film, Guido remains a fictional creation rather than an autobiographical stand-in for Fellini. Even those incidents in <u>8-1/2</u> which are drawn from Fellini's life are distorted as they are filtered through the creative process. Fellini makes no attempt to reproduce events from his life with anything like autobiographical fidelity. For instance, the Saraghina episode as it appears in the film is markedly different from the event from Fellini's youth upon which it is based. Fellini himself makes this same point in Solmi's book:

[4]Peter Harcourt, "The Secret Life of Federico Fellini," <u>Film Quarterly</u>, Vol. XIX, No. 3, p. 13.

'You must choose a profession you know well, and I
had thought of an art director, someone whose job
resembles mine. At the beginning it seemed too bold to
depict a film director. I knew that everyone would
identify the character with Federico Fellini himself,
that they would have talked about autobiography. Now it
is true that inevitably all the episodes in 8-1/2 refer
to my life, but some of them gradually became distorted,
while others took shape during the shooting. The result
was a story of a director who must begin a film but cannot remember the plot and continues to oscillate between
two planes: reality and imagination' (Solmi, p. 168).

This statement is further corroborated during an interview

between Deena Boyer and Fellini in which the director makes

it clear that the film is not his autobiography and that, in

fact, the decision to make the protagonist a film director

was a somewhat belated one. In fact, Fellini indicates that

he finally decided to make Guido a film director because that

is what he knew best, and not because he intended to make a

strictly autobiographical account of the difficulties which

he himself encountered during the making of 8-1/2 (Boyer,

pp. 10-11).

It is at this point, in fact, that the most crucial dif-

ference between Fellini and his protagonist becomes most

apparent. Acknowledging the autobiographical references

throughout the film, one must still concede that, in the end,

8-1/2 is, at most, a fictional correlative of Fellini's life.

Rather than writing his autobiography on film, Fellini pro-

jects certain of his experiences and problems, transposed

through the creative process, upon a fictional protagonist

who therefore resembles him in certain ways but is in no

sense identical to him. This is no more than most creative artists do; indeed, it is the keystone of the creative process. Fellini is no more identical to Guido than Joyce is identical to Daedelus, Hemingway is identical to Nick Adams, or Truffaut is identical to Antoine Doinel. One should not be misled by the fact that the protagonist of the film, like him, is a director, or that certain episodes in the film are drawn from his own experiences.

Unlike Fellini, however, Guido attempts to make a film autobiography rather than an autobiographical film. While Fellini creates, in 8-1/2, a correlative of his life on film, Guido hopes, in his film, to duplicate his life on celluloid. The roles, for instance, for which he casts actresses during the screen tests are autobiographical rather than fictional. Rather than being cast for fictional roles, they are being cast to play the people in his life. Similarly, Guido intends to recreate his childhood memories on film in strictly autobiographical terms, and discusses them as such with Daumier. Clearly he intends his film to be a faithful autobiographical account of the key moments of his entire life. He hopes to duplicate his experiences on film rather than using them as the basis for a creative fiction, which is Fellini's technique.

Thus, unlike Fellini, Guido is doomed to failure by the very nature of his enterprise. A quote by Max Beerbohm which appears in The Film Experience in a slightly different

context is illustrative in this regard. According to Beerbohm, "Life, save only through conventions is inimitable.
The more closely it be aped, the more futile and unreal its
copy."[5] Both critics and filmmakers alike have long recognized that reality, once filmed, is inevitably changed, both
because the mechanics of the cinema distort visual reality
and because the very act of filming somebody alters his
behavior. This latter fact is expressed most eloquently in
David Holzman's Diary by a character named Pepe:

> . . . You don't understand the basic principle: as
> soon as you start filming something, whatever happens in
> front of the camera is not reality any more. It becomes
> part of something else. It becomes a movie. And you
> stop living somehow. And you get very self-conscious
> about anything you do. 'Should I put my hand here?'
> 'Should I put my hand here?' 'Should I place myself
> this side of the frame?' 'Should I place myself this
> side of the frame?' And your decisions stop being moral
> decisions and become aesthetic decisions. And your
> whole life stops being your life and becomes a work of
> art--a very bad work of art this time. . . .[6]

Of course, Pepe's attack is directed towards cinéma
verité. It is just as applicable, if not more so, however,
to Guido's film. If reality eludes the practitioner of
cinéma verité, it most certainly will elude Guido. He
attempts to capture the reality of his life not by pointing a
camera at it but rather by replaying it with professional
actors. The fact that the actresses he tests become grotesque

[5] Roy Huss and Norman Silverstein, The Film Experience (New York, 1958), p. 152 n.

[6] L. M. Kit Carson, David Holzman's Diary (New York, 1970), pp. 47-48.

caricatures of the women he has known attests to the enormity
of his failure. After seeing them on the screen for the
first time he recognizes that his effort is doomed. A few
moments later his wife denounces his work as a lie. Stung by
the truth of her accusations he admits, for the first time in
8-1/2, that he cannot make his film. Later he confesses his
failure to Claudia.

The failure of Guido's enterprise, particularly in terms
of its faulty conception, thus represents, as Fellini himself
has indicated, the most crucial distinction between the fictional protagonist and the living artist. Guido fails because he does not understand the relationship between art and
reality, and specifically film and reality. There is no
sense in which he can be considered the author of 8-1/2, even
though certain scenes in 8-1/2 might coincide with the film
which he hopes to make. Guido fails to make his film, and,
in fact, this failure is crucial to the aesthetic statement
which is made in 8-1/2; namely that one cannot duplicate or
recreate reality in front of the camera. Guido does not
understand the nature of the cinema as does Fellini. He
fails where Fellini succeeds.

CHAPTER V

8-1/2 AND THE WORLD OF FELLINI'S FILMS

As is the case in the work of many great filmmakers, Fellini's work is pervaded by certain key themes and images which recur again and again to form a kind of personal mythology. 8-1/2 is very much a part of that mythology. Moreover, when viewed as a single entity, Fellini's films constitute nothing less than a massive assault upon some of the most cherished aspects of Italian society, particularly the Church and the spirit of machismo, the latter viewed particularly in terms of its degrading effect upon women. 8-1/2, as an important work within the Fellini canon, can certainly be viewed within the context of this assault.

The major themes which recur in Fellini's work must be viewed in the light of his social criticism. It is the one element common to all of Fellini's diverse concerns; including the corruption of religion, the crippling effects of guilt, the longing for purity, the grotesque decadence of modern life styles, the oppression of women in Italy, the archetypal similarities between life and the circus, and the need for personal liberation and self-knowledge. All of these themes are implicitly critical of Italian society.

166

Most of them appear in every Fellini film, and the extent to
which they are present in 8-1/2 defines its place within the
Fellini canon.

The overriding concern in 8-1/2 is Guido's need for the
self-knowledge necessary to transcend the artistic paralysis
which besets him. This concern about personal liberation,
however, is not restricted to 8-1/2. In fact, during the
"Long Interview" with Tullio Kezich, he says that it is a
fundamental theme in his work:

> Fellini: . . . We spend the second half of our lives
> wiping out the taboos, repairing the damage that educa-
> tion has caused in the first half. I'm speaking of men
> of my generation--I think this holds true for many.
> Kezich: It seems to me that this theme has dominated
> your recent films. La Dolce Vita approached it, in an
> emotional manner, in the episode of the meeting between
> Marcello and his father. 8-1/2, however, is a far
> clearer and more concise criticism of counterreformed
> education. And your Juliet is restrained as a human
> being within a debasing educational scheme; your film
> might be the story of her progressive liberation.
> Fellini: This is a fundamental theme for me, and I
> would like to go into it even more explicitly in the
> film I make after Juliet.[1]

Thus, not only is the theme of personal liberation seen by
the director as fundamental to his work, but, moreover, it
implies a rather stinging attack upon certain fundamental
aspects of Italian society. Often the strong need which many
of his characters have for personal liberation is experienced
as the need to liberate themselves from the oppressive

---

[1]Tullio Kezich and Federico Fellini, "The Long Interview," Juliet of the Spirits by Federico Fellini, trans.
Howard Greenfield (New York, 1965), p. 29.

influence of some aspect of Italian society, in this case the
Catholic educational system. This act of liberation becomes
the prerequisite to personal development.

In his early films, Fellini's attitude towards this
desire for self-liberation is not always consistent. In two
early films about provincials attempting to cope with the
mundane quality of their daily existence, The White Sheik
(1952) and I Vitelloni (1953), Fellini presents the theme of
personal liberation from two different perspectives. In the
first film he satirizes it, while in the second he seriously
confronts it. In the earlier film a provincial housewife,
bored with her commonplace existence, ludicrously seeks a
more exotic alternative in the world of fumetti models. Her
incredible naivite, particularly her inability at first to
perceive the tawdriness of the fumetti world, becomes the
object of Fellini's comedy. Yet, limited as the housewife's
perspective is, her attraction to the fumetti models is
motivated by a desire to transform her life. The fact that
she is attracted to such a shabby and farcical alternative
serves only to indicate the pathetic limitations of her provincial world view. I Vitelloni is about a group of young
men experiencing an unnaturally prolonged adolescence within
the confines of a provincial resort town during the off sea-
son. Unwilling to accept adult responsibilities in an environment which offers nothing in return, they remain aging
adolescents, and, in fact, are still treated like children by

heir parents. Adulthood, however, is represented only by
the dead-end street of a meaningless routine job. While most
of the men remain trapped in the provincial town at the end
of the film, Moraldo is able to liberate himself from the
confines of the provincial town, thus embracing the possibility of real growth and development. Unlike the housewife of
The White Sheik, there is a real sense in I Vitelloni that
Moraldo will be able to escape the emptiness of his provincial environment. His departure is a cause for hope rather
than for ridicule.

Although the housewife of The White Sheik becomes the
object of humor because of the limitations of her vision, a
crueler fate awaits those who are unable to transcend empty
and destructive modes of behavior. Self-knowledge for them
arrives too late, and only in a tragic context. In Il Bidone
(1955), for instance, Augusto's inability to forsake his
career as a swindler results in his brutal murder at the end
of the film. Earlier, in La Strada (1954), Zampano is unable
to grasp the destructive consequences of his animalistic
brutishness until confronted with the reality of Gelsomina's
death. If it can be said that he attains some sort of self-
knowledge at the end of the film, his enlightenment is tragi-
cally late. Just as we leave Augusto groveling on a hillside
listening to children's voices as he dies, we part with
Zampano as he grovels in the sand by the ocean while we hear
Gelsomina's theme playing in the background. The tragic and

ironic pattern of self-knowledge attained too late, suggested in these two endings, is one of Fellini's favorites, and it also reappears in 8-1/2 as has been pointed out earlier.

These early films generally deal with groups of relatively unsophisticated characters from the rural provinces of Italy, few of whom ever reflect in intellectual terms upon their condition. If a character, such as Moraldo, does attain some sort of self-awareness, he is not necessarily the central figure in the film. In later films, however, such as La Dolce Vita, 8-1/2, and Juliet of the Spirits, Fellini deals with one central figure of considerable complexity involved in an existential crisis which monopolizes our attention. Usually this crisis, in one form or another, involves the process of defining oneself which Jung refers to as individuation. All of these films, therefore, deal with a central existential crisis.

In La Dolce Vita, Marcello, the failed writer, seeks alternatives to the decadent life style into which he finds himself sinking. Most specifically, he seeks an alternative in the world of Steiner the intellectual, but his bitter disillusionment at Steiner's suicide only serves to accelerate the tailspin which has characterized his career throughout the film. At the end of the film Marcello is a defeated man, unable to rejoin the girl in white who, like Claudia in 8-1/2, represents a lost innocence to which he can no longer return. Although he attempts to define his role in a complex nd frightening world, his efforts are without success, and t the end of the film he is lost.

In 8-1/2, of course we see a similar process of self-definition conclude on an ambiguous, but still more positive note. In Juliet of the Spirits, Juliet, like Guido, undergoes a process of personal development in the Jungian mold. Like Guido she must liberate herself from the crippling influence of her Catholic education. Moreover, just as Guido has to liberate himself from the influence of his anima projections, she must liberate herself from the influence of her shadow projections, represented by Iris-Suzy-Fanny. Whereas Guido's process of liberation entails a reconciliation with those who populate his world, Juliet's liberation entails a separation from her domineering husband.

Even in Toby Dammit we find a man in frenzied pursuit of an alternate life style. Here Fellini presents us with a macabre inversion of one of his favorite motifs, the girl in white. Toby pursues his vision of a little girl in white, an image which seems to represent, as it does in La Dolce Vita and 8-1/2, an innocence which serves as an alternative to the phoney and decadent ambiance of show business. This time, however, Fellini inverts his traditional imagery, and the girl's satanic power lures Toby to his death. At the end she substitutes his freshly decapitated head for the white ball she had previously played with.

By now it is clear that the importance of self-knowledge

and personal liberation is a vital theme throughout Fellini's work. Often, as in 8-1/2 and Juliet of the Spirits, the chief obstacle to self-realization is the Church. Throughout his work, Fellini depicts the Church as a corrupt anachronism, an institution which oppresses people rather than liberating them.

There is, of course, a certain ambivalence in Fellini's depiction of the Church. We find, particularly in the early films in which his attitude towards the Church is more generous, that many of the clerics are good people. One remembers, for instance, the kindly nuns of La Strada. Until 8-1/2 and Juliet, in fact, clergymen are generally depicted in a positive light. Only in these latter two films does his attitude toward the Church become so bitter that even the clergy are tainted. This is because Fellini's primary target is usually the Church's doctrines and its immense power.

In many of the films this power is reflected in Fellini's depiction of the people's willingness to believe. Again and again they are swindled by con artists posing as clergymen or religious visionaries. In Il Bidone, the swindlers' most successful ploy is to dress like clergymen. In this way they effortlessly bilk credulous peasants of their savings. In both The Nights of Cabiria and La Dolce Vita, bogus miracles provide the pretext for swindling the credulous masses. It is an easy matter for the con men to move onto the Church's turf, for the Church itself has long been a heavily commercial enterprise. Thus, the people have come to expect the inevitable appeal for funds which is part of both the priest's and con man's game.

In La Strada, Fellini's attitude towards the Church seems to be more positive, but even here the institution is subjected to at least gentle mockery. At one of the most desperate moments in Gelsomina's career, when she seems lost in the Italian countryside, a band of clowns materializes playing a tune on their musical instruments. She follows them, and they lead her into a provincial town. Immediately the film cuts to a church procession within the town. The music which accompanies the procession, this time slower and more stately, is the same tune played by the clowns. Musically, Fellini equates the church procession to the clowns who parade through the countryside.

In his later films, however, Fellini's mockery is much less gentle. In The Temptation of Dr. Antonio, 8-1/2 and Juliet of the Spirits Fellini is critical of the puritanical Catholic attitude towards sex and its effect on Italians. In the person of Doctor Antonio, the licentious censor, the perverse lust which underlies all puritanism is parodied. 8-1/2, however, takes a much grimmer view of the psychological legacy of the Church's repressive attitudes, and Juliet of the Spirits is even more critical. Not only do the Church's sexual mores impose the same feelings of guilt upon Juliet that Guido experiences, but, beyond this, by abetting the old moral double standard they serve to legitimize her subservient role within her marriage.

In both these films the Church's most powerful weapon is guilt. Fellini is deeply concerned with the role of guilt in modern society, and nowhere is this more apparent than in his imaginative recreation of the Roman past, Fellini Satyricon. Here Fellini attempts to recreate a society which predated the Christian concept of guilt. At the same time, this ancient society is also Fellini's vision of the post-Christian society which he now sees as emerging in the West. Here then is a world of unbridled passions, steeped in a hedonism undiluted by any Catholic misgivings. It is a powerful work of the imagination attempting to recreate a state of mind and a life style which has long since disappeared in the West but which, paradoxically, may be re-emerging again. The difference between the moral ambiance of Satyricon and that of Fellini's earlier films defines the parameters of the Church's power in Italy as Fellini views it. In a sense, the brutality of Satyricon's world implies a nostalgia for certain Christian values worth maintaining while others must be discarded and suggests a final ambivalence in Fellini's attitude towards Catholic morality.

It is clear, however, that the Church is no longer relevant to people's needs in the contemporary era. Perhaps the most striking image of this in Fellini's films is that of the statue of Christ in La Dolce Vita absurdly dangling from a

helicopter as it flies over the fleshpots of Rome. Later, of
course, in 8-1/2, the chief representative of the Church is a
senile Cardinal who is totally incapable of relating to the
world around him.

In Juliet of the Spirits the Church is also one of the
societal forces which conspires to maintain women in a subservient position. The inferior status of women in Italian
society, moreover, is a consistent concern in Fellini's work,
and, in fact, his films constitute an ongoing attack upon the
Latin code of machismo. It is no accident that a large number of Fellini's leading ladies are loving and passive, while
many of his leading men are cruel and aggressive.

Often Fellini's women are victimized either by the brutality of men or by the hostile ambiance of their culture.
Certainly the most famous example of the former case is the
brutal mistreatment of Gelsomina by Zampano in La Strada.
The full extent of her oppression is revealed when the Fool
has to convince her that she has some basic worth as a human
being:

> Il Matto: . . . I don't know what it's good for, this
> pebble, but it certainly has its use! If it were use-
> less, then everything else would also be useless--even
> the stars! That's the way things are, you know. You
> too, you too have reason for being here, with your
> artichoke head.[2]

Cabiria is similar to Gelsomina in her need to extend
love to others, but her needs are denied with equal cruelty.

[2]Federico Fellini, scene from La Strada in Gilbert
Salacha's Federico Fellini (New York, 1970), p. 129.

In order to express her love, she becomes a prostitute, because men seem unwilling to accept her love on any other
basis (Budgen, pp. 21-24). Throughout the film, she is subjected to the brutality of a series of men, including the
last one who promises to marry her in order to steal her
money.

Married women in Fellini's films seldom fare any better
than these unfortunate ladies. Almost always, it is the men
who cuckold their wives; women seem incapable of adultery.
Sandra, in I Vitelloni, is naively oblivious of her husband's
extramarital adventures. Luisa, in 8-1/2, could hardly be
described as naive or oblivious to her husband's extramarital
activity, but she is incapable of betraying Guido, even when
the opportunity presents itself. Juliet's husband goes one
step further than the other men discussed here, for he de-
serts her. In the sudden absence of her husband she is panic
stricken, for she feels she has no identity apart from him.
Here there is a direct connection between her religious conditioning and her pitiful subservience, and at the end of the
film she quite literally frees herself from the bonds of this
conditioning, untying the child from the burning rack, so
that she will be able to define herself on her own terms.

Often in Fellini's films, with the singular exception of
Juliet of the Spirits, his men come to understand the cruelty
of their actions. Both Fausto and Guido learn that they
really love their wives, although for Guido, unlike Fausto,

this insight comes too late to save his marriage. Similarly,
Zampano comes to recognize the consequences of his brutality
too late to change anything or save anyone.

Clearly, salvation and redemption are important ideals
in Fellini's work. His films are inherently moralistic.
Those who have wronged others, such as Fausto, Augusto,
Zampano, or Guido must come to learn the error of their ways.
Those who are innocent, but have been wronged, such as
Sandra, Gelsomina, Cabiria, and Juliet, must be given suffi-
cient hope to continue living. Only with Gelsomina does this
pattern falter at the end.

Salvation, redemption, and hope, however, are not represented by the Church in Fellini's work. Often, in fact, they
are represented by the circus, particularly by its clowns.
In La Strada, for instance, when Gelsomina seems lost in the
Italian countryside a band of clowns appears to lead her
towards the city and to renew her spirits. Moreover, throughout the film, the Fool serves to instill in her some sense of
her worth as a human being. At the end of 8-1/2, the band of
clowns who initiate Guido's final redemption fantasy are a
reprise of the clowns in La Strada.

Clowns become redemptive figures because the circus,
unlike the Church, is associated with life itself, both in
terms of the beautiful and the grotesque. This is clearly
implied by the fact that the final scene of 8-1/2, in which
Guido is reunited with all the people he has known, takes

place inside a circus ring. Here life literally becomes a circus. Furthermore, with a respect to his clowns, Fellini devotes the opening section of his film essay The Clowns to a demonstration that circus clowns have their counterparts in life and that, in fact, the line which differentiates the grotesques we find in life from the grotesques we find among the clowns is rather blurred. Much the same point is made in La Strada when Fellini equates the church procession to the band of clowns. In Satyricon, Fellini depicts the ancient world as if it were populated with his clowns, so that the film abounds with leering grotesques in painted faces.

In this last film, of course, the clown is hardly a redemptive figure. He serves, rather, as a grotesque carica-ture of the passions, violence, and lust which are repressed in our modern Christian world. In this sense the clowns of Satyricon are very much like the clowns we see at the begin-ning of The Clowns when Fellini, as a young boy, is fright-ened by the exaggerated violence of their antics. By the end of the film, of course, the clown is revealed to be a prac-ticioner of a fine, if dying art, and the film closes with two clowns playing the trumpet, a scene which recalls the clown bands of earlier films.

While the circus, in Fellini's idiosyncratic world, comes to represent qualities conventionally associated with the Church, it cannot serve as a source of metaphysics or ethics. As Fellini's view of the Church becomes increasingly

more bitter in his later films, his world becomes increasingly devoid of any moral standard upon which to base one's
actions. Thus Marcello, Guido, Juliet, and Toby Dammit
search desperately for some basis for action in a world in
which the Church is an anachronism. Satyricon is the logical
consequence of this evolution, for here Fellini suggests the
possible moral evolution of the Western world after the
demise of Christian values by portraying the West as he imagines it before they arose. The vision is fundamentally
ambivalent, for although he clearly disapproves of the repressive character of the Church, the hedonistic and violent
world he envisions in its absence is not a particularly
appealing alternative.

By now it should be clear that Fellini deals with the
same set of themes throughout all of his films. The emphasis
changes from time to time, and Fellini's attitude towards his
basic material shifts, as can be seen in the progressive
hardening of his judgment of the Church, but essentially the
development of his themes is not pronounced. In contrast to
this, however, the development of style in Fellini is much
more dramatic. The stylistic context within which Fellini
creates his personal mythology changes radically with time.
This is most evident in the treatment of point of view in his
films.

In his early period, Fellini confines his camera to the
surface of physical reality and typically deals with a group

of major characters operating basically within the confines
of the real world. This is generally the stylistic format o
all the films which range from Variety Lights to La Dolce
Vita. Then, beginning with The Temptation of Dr. Antonio, a
new pattern is initiated. Fellini moves more directly towar
a first-person narrative, focusing upon a single major character who dwarfs all others in importance, and moving inside
his head to portray his inner fantasies and dreams directly
on the screen. This first-person format is maintained in
8-1/2, Juliet of the Spirits, and Toby Dammit. Perhaps La
Dolce Vita and Nights of Cabiria could be seen as transitional films, in this pattern, at least with respect to the con-
centration on one central figure. They do not, however, portray the fantasy lives of their protagonists directly on the
screen.

Finally, Fellini's most recent films present a new facet
of his development. Rather than presenting the fantasies of
his fictional characters on the screen, he now presents his
own fantasies directly on the screen. Although Satyricon
deals with an ancient historical period and The Clowns and
Fellini's Roma are essays set in the contemporary world,
rather than works of narrative fiction, all of these films
are really direct projections of Fellini's own fantasy life.

Satyricon, for instance, is an imaginative re-creation
of the spirit and ambiance of the pre-Christian world, not an
attempt to re-create ancient history. The setting of the fil
seldom bears any physical correspondence to the ancient world

ecause the film is really set in Fellini's mind. The
xpressionistic settings and costumes in the film are a
irect reflection of his imagined sense of the ambiance of
he ancient world. The unbridled lust and violence which
haracterize interpersonal relationships reflect his imagined
ense of morality, or the lack of it, in the pre-Christian
orld.

Similarly, neither The Clowns nor Fellini's Roma is an
ttempt to depict contemporary realities with the realism of
a documentary. Rather, they are film essays in which Fellini
resents directly upon the screen his feelings, memories, and
fantasies about the circus and Rome. Thus, as his films
volve, Fellini moves more and more deeply into his own fantasies, and in his latest films merely dispenses with the
contrivance of attributing them to various fictional protagonists. He has begun to create essays about his own view of
both the past and the present, and it is no accident, therefore, that the titles of two of these films bear his name.

APPENDIX A

A SYNOPSIS OF <u>8-1/2</u>*

Scene 1: The film opens in an underground traffic tunnel
jammed with cars unable to move. The tunnel is dim, but the
light at the entrance is highly intense. Guido is dreaming
that he is trapped within this traffic jam and that his car
is rapidly filling up with deadly white fumes. He claws
frantically at the windows, which are locked tight, as he
attempts to escape. Motorists in other cars watch his struggle impassively showing no concern for his plight. In a car
to the rear of Guido's, a lecherous old man paws a younger
lady, Guido's mistress, Carla, whom we will later meet in the
film. Passengers hang out of the windows of a bus like meat.
The only sound is Guido's heavy and frantic breathing and the
sound of his fingers scraping against the glass. At the last
moment he is able to force a window open. He crawls out upon
the roof and begins to float upward away from the car and out
of the tunnel. He soars upward towards the clouds which
swirl about him in the heavy wind. His back is to the camera, as it has been from the first moment of this scene. We
never see his face. As he soars through the clouds, we see,
for a brief moment, a shot of the launching tower which he is
erecting on a beach as a gigantic prop for his next film.
The overall feeling is now one of exhilaration.

*The film has been divided into scenes according to
natural transitions in the action.

183

18

The film now cuts to a shot of a horseman riding across a beach in the dazzling white heat of the midday sun. He approaches another man lying on his stomach upon the sand an holding a string leading up towards the sky as if attached t a kite. Later in the film we shall meet the horseman again as Claudia's manager and the man on the beach as Claudia's press agent. The man on the beach says, "I've got him," and gets up. The film then cuts to a subjective shot from Guido's point of view as he hovers in the sky, high over the beach. His leg is now tied to the rope held by Claudia's press agent, and Guido frantically attempts to remove it. The horseman orders him brought down, and suddenly Guido plummets from the sky into the sea below. A breathless gasp is heard.

Scene 2: Close-up of a hand reaching frantically into the air in a darkened room. The gasp of fear covers the transition from the fall to this shot, and is reminiscent of gasping sounds which Guido also makes when he is trapped in the car filling up with gas. Now, however, it is clear that Guido has woken from the nightmare sequence which opened the film. Guido, still in bed, is then interrogated by a doctor who proceeds to give him a physical examination. Throughout most of the scene we only see various parts of Guido's body and never his face. Daumier enters and waits to speak with Guido. The doctor asks him about his film and the pictures

of actresses scattered about his bed. As the examination
concludes, Guido gets out of bed and stumbles towards the
camera. For the first time we see his weathered face. He
enters the bathroom, stares at his face, a portrait of
exhaustion, in the mirror and turns on the bright bathroom
lights. They flicker on, and the dazzling brightness contrasts with the darkness of the bedroom. A telephone rings
and Guido bends comically before another, larger mirror,
holding his back and caricaturing the infirmities of old age.
In the background we hear Wagner's "Valkyrie" theme.

Scene 3: The film cuts to the long circular pan, described
in detail earlier, of the garden of the spa. The "Valkyrie"
theme grows louder in the background providing a transition
between scenes, and the bright lighting of the white bathroom
continues to fill the screen in the form of the dazzling sun-
shine which pervades the garden. After the series of complex
establishing shots of the garden, described earlier, the camera rests upon a close-up of Guido waiting in line for a drink
from the fountain at the spa. The "Valkyrie" theme has been
supplanted by the overture to "The Barber of Seville." Suddenly Guido looks towards the camera and pulls his glasses
down the bridge of his nose. The music stops. We see Claudia
in the distance beyond the fountain area. She runs toward the
camera, her arms flung back. We have now obviously entered
Guido's imagination. She seems to float towards the camera,

and when she reaches the fountain area she offers Guido a
glass of mineral water. As the camera cuts to a close-up of
Guido and he thanks her, we hear a somewhat harsh female
voice impatiently asking him to take his water. The film
cuts to a shot of a rather unattractive female attendant, in
Claudia's place, offering Guido a glass of water.

Guido takes the glass and, as he walks away from the
fountain, meets Daumier. Daumier gives him some notes he has
made containing his impression of the proposed film. They
walk together and Daumier continues to speak critically of
the film and asks Guido why he hired him to assist on the
script. At this point Guido spots an old friend, Mario
Mezzabotta, an older man in his fifties. He, in turn, introduces Guido to Gloria, his young, intellectual fiance.
Daumier joins them, and as the group continues to talk together, Guido leaves them and begins reading Daumier's notes.
We hear the sound of his interior voice over the sound track
as he reads Daumier's notes, which criticize the introduction
into the film of the girl in white, Claudia, whom we have
seen, as she appeared in Guido's mind, only moments before.

Scene 4: A small railroad station. Guido is seated on a
bench still reading Daumier's notes as he waits for a train
to arrive. His interior voice is still heard, a transitional
device linking this setting to the preceding scene. The
train arrives, and Guido is unable to spot the person he is

waiting for. He is about to leave, apparently relieved, when he sees his mistress, Carla, emerging from behind the far side of the departing train. She is ostentatiously over-dressed, wearing furs at the height of the hot Italian sum-mer. They meet and Guido informs her that she will be unable to stay at his hotel. He assures her, however, that he has found a nice place for her to stay. They leave the station.

Scene 5: The dining room of Carla's hotel. Through the win-dows we can see that the midday sun, which filled the spa and flooded the entrance to the railroad station, is still shin-ing brightly. The light in the dining room, however, is dim-mer than in the previous two scenes. While Carla washes her hands, Guido talks to the lady in charge of the hotel. She is impressed by Carla's furs. Guido then joins Carla in the washroom. As they talk, we hear, in the background, the sound of a woman humming tunes which, as was explained earlier, are associated with Guido's boyhood memories. The woman's sing-ing clearly exists only in Guido's imagination. It briefly ceases, but resumes for a few moments while Carla and Guido are eating. Guido is clearly bored with Carla's endless chatter, and mimics the jabbering of her voice. He shows interest only when she tells of her dream of her husband mur-dering them.

Scene 6: The back of Carla's head as she stands in front of a window. The light outdoors now is dim. The screen is

dark, reflecting the dimness of her bedroom. Guido asks her
to close the curtain. She does, and the room is darkened
further. Guido makes Carla up to look like a whore, and he
asks her to leave the room and re-enter as if she were entering the wrong room and discovering a stranger in bed. After
she exits, however, voices are heard in the hall. She
returns, having forgotten her part, and tells Guido that the
hotel owner offered her mineral water. Then she opens the
towel which has been wrapped around her body and falls upon
Guido, who is lying in bed. "Do you love me a little?" she
asks.

Scene 7: Later in the same bedroom. Carla is propped up in
bed reading a comic book and giggling while Guido sleeps beside her. The only light in the room is the lamp on the
table next to Carla. Guido dreams that an older woman enters
the room, her back to the camera, and begins to rub the wall
in a circular motion with a cloth, as if she were attempting
to polish it. We cut to a close-up from behind the woman.
The screen suddenly brightens and the woman is now polishing
a window. Behind her, reflected in the glass, stands Guido
dressed in his schoolboy uniform. Guido catches a glimpse of
his father walking quickly behind the wall lining one side of
the cemetery. Guido follows him into his tomb. Inside,
Guido's father complains about the size of his crypt.
Guido's producer and Conocchia arrive, express their

dissatisfaction with Guido, and then leave. Guido then helps his father as he lowers himself back down into the earth. Then Guido and his mother exchange light goodby kisses. Suddenly she grips him and kisses him passionately on the lips. When they break apart she has been transformed into Guido's wife, Luisa. Guido stares at her, astonished by the transformation, and Luisa mockingly asks him if he has forgotten her. The film then cuts to an aerial view of the entire cemetery, described earlier. Far below, Luisa stands alone. Guido has vanished from sight. Luisa, downcast in the empty cemetery, seems the embodiment of despair. The dream ends.

Scene 8: A dim hotel corridor. Guido walks towards the camera humming a carefree tune and hopping occasionally to the beat. He buzzes for an elevator and when it arrives he enters. In the elevator is the Cardinal, the priest, and the layman who accompanies them. Guido's carefree mood is immediately dampened. The camera cuts from Guido to the prelates and their assistant. The faces of the prelates are dramatically highlighted against the dark background of the elevator.

Scene 9: The lobby of Guido's hotel. It is clearly daytime, and the lobby is brightly lit. Guido exits from the elevator and is confronted by a variety of his associates who harass him about his projected film. Much of this action is encompassed in the complex opening traveling shot described earlier. One of the people who badger him is Claudia's manager,

who asks him about her part in the film. We have seen him
earlier as the horseman on the beach in the nightmare which
opened the film. Guido briefly breaks away from his tormen-
tors to greet the French actress who is to play his mother in
the film. Claudia's agent then returns to ask him, once
again, about the script. While they are talking Guido
catches a glimpse of a rather mysterious lady, played by
Caterina Boratto, who continues to attract him throughout the
film. Here she is walking across the lobby with her young
daughter. Guido is then badgered by an American reporter and
his wife. Finally, Cesarino, his assistant, convinces him to
cast an old man for the part of his father in the film.

Cesarino introduces Guido to three old men vying for the
part of his father. Guido, whose temper has flared earlier
in the scene at Conocchia, is now visibly edgy and rejects
all three men as not being old enough for the part. Cesarino
protests, but Guido turns from him and walks off chanting
incoherently in the Eastern style. The sudden change in
Guido's behavior is immediately apparent. Guido's producer,
Pace, is seen descending the long stairway to the lobby with
his young girl friend. Guido kneels at the foot of the stairs
before him as before an oriental potentate. He is still
chanting. The producer bids him to rise and presents him
with a watch as a gift.

Scene 10: Nighttime at the spa's night club. The scene

opens with a close-up of the profile of an elderly German
songstress, silhouetted against a spotlight. The night club
is filled with elderly people who dance slowly while she
sings. The music speeds up and we cut to a shot of Gloria
and Mezzabotta dancing. He is sweating heavily while trying
to keep up with the pace she sets. At one point she dances
in an oriental style which recalls Guido's chanting in the
previous scene. Guido watches them, a bemused expression on
his face. He taps a long nose made of dough which he has
molded over his own nose. Guido's associates at the table
make small talk which seems to bore Guido. Carla enters the
night club and sits at a table by herself. She slyly blows
Guido a kiss, and he is visibly disconcerted by her presence.
Conocchia and Pace discuss the cost of the spaceship being
built for the film, and Guido grows even more uncomfortable.
The French actress' agent asks him how many scenes she will
be in. Guido says that she will be in five scenes. The
actress is visibly upset, while Daumier laughs heartily.

Bruno, Guido's second assistant, informs him that Mezzabotta is making a pass at Carla. Guido assents to his suggestion that he dance with her. The French actress complains
that she knows nothing of her role, and Guido tells her that
it is not necessary for her to know anything. Mezzabotta
approaches Guido, still sweating heavily. He squats down to
talk to Guido, panting heavily like a dog. Gloria returns to
her chair on the opposite side of the table. She picks up a

bunch of cherries and exclaims pretentiously that they "look
like glass." She then tosses some to Mezzabotta and Guido.

Mezzabotta and Guido walk from the table. Mezzabotta
asks Guido what he thinks about his relationship with Gloria.
He asks Guido, "Now tell me the truth, am I a fool?" Before
Guido can answer, they are interrupted by the French actress'
manager, who demands a shooting schedule. Guido turns to the
actress and tells her that she looks like a snail, referring
to her hat decked with two snail-like antennas. She seems
hurt, apparently taking the remark as a personal criticism,
until Guido indicates that he is referring to her hat.

Suddenly the film cuts to the stage of the night club.
A figure stands outlined in the darkness. The spotlight
flares on revealing Maurice the magician, dressed in tuxedo
and top hat. His face is incredibly pale and seems almost to
be a death mask. At first he holds up items belonging to
various women at the night club while his blindfolded assistant, Maya, announces the identity of whatever object he picks
up. He then begins to transmit the thoughts of various
people at the night club to her. When he approaches Carla's
table and offers to read her mind, Guido becomes visibly
nervous. Maurice then approaches the table at which Guido
and his associates are sitting. He attempts to read Gloria's
thoughts but she begins screaming hysterically for him to go
away. She then runs into the arms of Mezzabotta, who leads
her away. The group begins to leave the table but Maurice

follows them. He speaks to Guido, and it turns out that they
know each other. Maurice transmits Guido's thoughts to Maya
and she writes the words "ASA NISI MASA" on the blackboard.
Maurice asks Guido if she is correct, and Guido nods yes.
"What does it mean?" exclaims Maurice.

Scene 11:   The farmhouse of Guido's childhood memories. It
is dimly lit but still brighter than the night club. A young
boy, Guido, crawls under a table to escape the clutches of a
family nurse. Finally, after running through the house, he
is caught and carried to a huge vat in which he is bathed,
with many other young children in a vat of wine lees. He is
then wrapped in a towel and carried upstairs to bed by one of
the nurses. After the nurses have closed the door on him and
the other children, a girl in the bed opposite his sits up
and tells him that on this particular night a magic incanta-
tion can make the eyes of a man in an old painting on the
wall move and point the way to buried treasure. She then begins to gesture mysteriously and chant the magic words, "ASA
NISI MASA." The film then cuts to a montage of the farmhouse
at night, culminating in a close-up of the fire in the hearth.
The only sound is the wind whistling through the courtyard.
Dissolve.

Scene 12:   The hotel lobby at night. The lighting is dim.
The hotel manager tells Guido that his wife called earlier
and then has his operator return the call. Guido walks

through the lobby and spots the mystery lady on the telephone. She tearfully tells the person she is talking to that she forgives him for everything. Guido pauses and then moves on. The French actress asks to talk to him, and offers him a drink. She then attempts to seduce him, but Guido is disinterested and resists her rather crude advances. She becomes distraught and exclaims pleadingly, "I'm a very sensual woman." Guido, however, is already leaving to speak to his wife on the phone.

Guido picks up the telephone near the reception desk and speaks to Luisa. She asks where he has been all night and he explains that he has been hard at work. Filled with guilt, Guido invites Luisa to join him at the spa. As Guido leaves the telephone booth after the conversation, the French actress calls to him once again but he ignores her. The camera pans up to a clock over the stairway leading to the lobby. It is two A.M.

Scene 13: A subjective shot as the door opens and the camera, in Guido's place, enters the production room. Even at this late hour Guido's assistants are hard at work. After discussing some aspects of the production with Bruno, he discovers that Cesarino has been in bed, at the back of the room, with two young girls. One of the girls says that her friend says that Guido can't make a good love story. Guido answers that she is right.

Upon leaving the production room, Guido encounters Conocchia in the hallway outside, waiting for him. Conocchia complains that Guido is ignoring him, and Guido angrily calls him an "old fool." Conocchia, deeply hurt, begins to weep. Conocchia continues to berate him, and before entering his room warns Guido that he had better be careful because he is not the man he used to be. Guido, who has been sitting on the floor, gets up and enters his room.

Scene 14: Guido's room. Extremely dark. Guido enters the room. On the sound track we can hear his thoughts as he worries that Conocchia might be right about him losing his creative talent. In his imagination he sees Claudia, his muse, enter the room from behind a curtain. He seems surprised at her appearance. He enters the bathroom and slumps wearily on a bench. The bathroom is brightly lit, which sets it off dramatically from the rest of the room. Guido pours a bottle of hair tonic over his head and seems disillusioned even with Claudia as he says, "Enough of these escapist themes." The film cuts between him in the bathroom and Claudia awaiting him in the room. While she wore a white uniform when she entered the room, she is now wearing only a slip.

Guido leaves the bathroom more hopeful. He speculates on the possibility of making Claudia a museum curator's daughter. Claudia looks at his script and laughs. Guido, discouraged, says that she is right to laugh at him, and somersaults headfirst onto his bed covered with photographs of young starlets. Claudia attempts to console him, kissing him on the hands and lips. She lowers the strap of her slip. In the next shot we see her lying in bed, the sheets pulled to her chin. Over and over she repeats, "I want to create order, I want to create cleanliness."

A telephone rings. The spell of Guido's daydream is broken. He is lying in bed, his head at the foot of the bed and the picture of a young actress propped up against the pillow between his feet. Here the return to reality is indicated partly by the reversal of Guido's position on the bed. During the daydream he lay with his head on the pillow.

Guido picks up the phone. It is Carla who is sick in bed at her hotel. She implores Guido to come right over.

Scene 15: Carla's room, brighter than Guido's. She is feverish and is sweating profusely. Guido places a damp rag across her forehead and attempts to comfort her. In her fever, her deep-seated doubts and fears about their relationship rise to the surface. She asks Guido why he stays with her. Guido does not answer her. Sitting on the bed, he is preoccupied by other thoughts. We hear his interior voice as he thinks, "What am I going to say to the Cardinal tomorrow?"

Scene 16: Midday in the garden of the spa. Brighter than Carla's room. We hear Guido discussing his script as the

camera moves through the garden in a subjective shot. Guido
is walking with the Cardinal's lay representative and discussing his film script with him. They are joined by the
priest and continue to discuss the script. At the far end of
the garden, the Cardinal awaits them seated on a chair. The
camera dollies in on him as Guido draws closer and he looks
up to greet the director.

At the beginning of the audience the Cardinal questions
Guido about his personal life. He asks whether Guido has any
children and, in a revealing slip of the tongue, Guido answers
that he does. Then he hastily corrects himself. The Cardinal,
rather than discuss the religious aspects of Guido's film,
drifts off into a commentary upon the significance of the
song of the Diomedes bird, which we hear in the background.
Guido gazes about in boredom and catches a glimpse of an
enormously heavy woman trudging down a hill behind him. He
pulls his glasses down the bridge of his nose and stares at
her.

Scene 17: The schoolyard of Guido's memory. The lighting is
dazzlingly bright. In the schoolyard a group of students in
their uniforms are playing soccer. Guido is among them, and
from a wall overlooking the yard a group of boys call to him
to join them. After a moment's hesitation he does join them
and they run off to a rendevouz with Saraghina at the beach.
Flushed out of the old pill box in which she lives by the

boys, Saraghina dances for them after they pay her. She is
an enormous mountain of flesh, like the woman who appears at
the end of the previous scene. Near the conclusion of her
dance she picks Guido up and dances with him. Two clerics
appear and, after a short chase, capture Guido.

We cut to the seminary. Guido is judged by a tribunal
of priests. His mother, who sits in one corner of the room,
refuses to comfort him. He is forced to wear a dunce cap in
his classes and eat off the floor of the dining room. Later
we find him on the way to confession. On the way he is
frightened by a mummified figure inside of a glass case. The
figure, perhaps a saint, is grotesquely ravaged by decay, and
Fellini's camera lingers on its mouldering face.

The camera dollies in on a dark confessional booth which
seems to float within the whiteness of the room. The priest
inside tells Guido that Saraghina is the devil. As they exit
there is a shot of the statue of the Virgin Mary which resembles the mystery lady at the hotel. In a dissolve it is
superimposed momentarily upon the pill box in which Saraghina
lives. Guido returns to the beach. He kneels on the sand
and waves his cap at Saraghina who smiles and says "Ciao."
Dissolve.

Scene 18: The dining room of Guido's hotel. The Cardinal
and his clerical companions are seated at a table. It is not

quite as brightly lit as the beach. Daumier criticizes the scene we have just seen as sentimental and meaningless. He urges Guido to eliminate it from his film. Thus, Guido's memories are translated into projected scenes for his new film when we return to the real world. Thus, they serve a dual purpose in 8-1/2. As he begins to finish his critique, Daumier gets up and walks away from the table, still talking. He walks past a fat lady who is singing while another plays the piano.

Scene 19: The film cuts to a band dressed in white playing furiously in front of a large bright window. As the music plays in the background men and women wrapped in towels walk down separate sets of stairs towards the steam baths underneath the spas. Guido and his producer descend the stairs. On the way down Guido notices the mystery lady on the women's stairway. Then he enters the steam bath with his producer. The steam bath is inhabited by old men wrapped in towels and, as they wander through the rising clouds of steam, it takes on the atmosphere of a kind of inferno.

Guido sits on a bench and notices Mezzabotta sitting beside him. He speaks to Mezzabotta, but the aged diplomat does not respond. The camera pans along the benches upon which the old men are slumped and then cuts to a close-up of Guido. A towel is draped over his head and the camera moves in slowly to a tight shot of his glasses fogged over by steam.

The scene now moves from reality to fantasy. Guido imagines that he hears the voice of an airline stewardess, a figure from a past love affair who surfaces in the harem fantasy. She announces that the Cardinal is waiting for him. Guido gets up and hurries out of the steam room. As he rushes to his audience, his associates rush up to him, hand him his clothes, and plead for special favors. All of this activity is accomplished in one long, complex shot described earlier.

Guido enters a dark sub-basement room. A casement window above him opens. Through the window Guido sees the Cardinal sitting in a chair. A towel is draped around him, and for a moment we see his profile silhouetted against the towel. Guido tells the Cardinal he is not happy and the Cardinal asks why he should be happy. As the Cardinal walks across the room and immerses himself in a mud bath, he mutters irrelevent banalities in Latin. Over and over he repeats, "There is no salvation outside the Church." The camera draws back out of the window and, as we begin hearing the tune of "Blue Moon" in the background, the window closes.

Scene 20: The music of "Blue Moon" provides a transition to this scene and is still heard in the background. It is dusk and crowds of people are hurrying past a modern arcade. Inside various activities take place. An auction is being

held. A fakir sleeps on a bed of nails within a glass case.
Luisa, Guido's wife, walks through the crowd. She is being
followed by Guido, who bites his nails nervously. Looking
back for a second, she sees him and does a double take. He
greets her and they meet in front of a painting of the ocean
crashing upon the surf. Both of them seem pleased by the
reunion as they walk off toward the outdoor cafe.

Scene 21: Nighttime. Guido and Luisa are dancing at the
outdoor cafe. They bump into Enrico, one of Luisa's companions, who is dancing with Tina, another friend of Luisa's.
Guido asks Luisa if Enrico is a bit in love with her. This
remark pleases her and she dances off teasingly by herself.
The producer appears and greets Luisa. Rosella, Luisa's best
friend, joins them. The producer invites them all out to see
the launching tower he is constructing for Guido's film.
Luisa seems to wander off, and as the group of people head
for cars, Guido walks with Rosella. She tells him how happy
Luisa is that Guido has invited her to the spa. When they
enter the cars, however, Guido notices that Luisa is standing
alone and downcast. He calls to her and she reluctantly
joins them, but gets into the front seat of the car rather
than sitting in the back with Guido.

Scene 22: In the darkness of night, a group of cars
approaches the launching tower, which is dramatically lit
against the black sky. Following the producer, his entourage

leave their cars and follow him up the stairs leading to the
higher levels of the tower. On one level Enrico and Luisa
pause for a moment. Enrico offers her his coat and attempts
to cheer her up. An airplane roars overhead, drowning out
the sound track.

On the ground below the tower, Rosella and Guido have
paused to speak to each other. They talk about the film, and
Guido tells her that in his film everything happens. He
tells her that even an old sailor working on the set will be
in the film. He then asks the sailor to dance, but after a
couple of minutes, when the sailor's singing and dancing become an annoyance, he brutally orders him to stop.

Guido says that he can't understand what his wife wants
from him, and Rosella answers that she wants him to be different from what he is. The conversation slowly shifts from
Guido's marriage to his film, and Guido confesses his creative impotence. "I have nothing to say," he says and then
sings, "but I want to say it just the same." He asks for
advice from Rosella's spirits. She says, "They say that you
are free. But you have to choose and you don't have much
time left. You have to choose soon." The camera pans up the
launching tower. From above the producer shouts, "Guido, are
you coming up or not?"

Scene 23: Guido is lying in his dim bedroom, a worried expression on his face. As Luisa enters he turns off the light

and pretends that he is asleep. Luisa enters, and surreptitiously dials a number, but nobody answers. She then gets into the other twin bed. She begins to read but then bursts out in laughter. Guido asks her why she is laughing and she answers that she could never be unfaithful to him because she couldn't stand the stupidity of having to hide and lie. Guido tries to ignore her but is unable to, and they begin to argue violently about their marriage and his affairs. Finally Luisa asks him why he brought her to the spa. "What do you want from me?" she cries, and we recall that in the previous scene Guido asked Rosella what Luisa wants from him. Luisa then rolls over in bed and goes to sleep. As the camera draws away from the twin beds, Guido and Luisa sleep with their backs to each other.

Scene 24: The open-air cafe near the spa. The dazzling brightness of the sun contrasts sharply with the darkness of Guido's room in the previous scene. Whiteness is the dominant motif of this scene. Guido, Luisa, and Rosella are seated at a table when Carla enters the restaurant. Carla, spotting them, hesitates momentarily and then sits down at a table at the other end of the cafe. Guido attempts to hide behind his newspaper, but Luisa tells him not to worry because she spotted Carla when she first arrived at the spa. For the first time we discover the motivation for her sudden change of mood the previous night. Luisa begins to berate

Guido more violently, particularly after Guido denies having
known that Carla was at the spa. She concludes by saying,
"What really nauseates me is that she knows everything about
our life."

Guido, however, begins to retreat within the safety of
his fantasy world. He slides back in his chair with a smile
on his face and says, "And yet." At this moment the film
moves into Guido's imagination. Carla begins to sing an absurdly operatic bit of music and Luisa rushes over to compli-
ment her on her singing, and she tells her that she has been
wanting to meet Carla for a long time. They kiss each other
and Guido applauds. Then, as they begin walking back towards
Guido, they begin to dance. Dissolve.

Scene 25: A fire burning in a hearth. Hands reach down and
take the pot from the fire. It is Luisa. Somehow she now
seems to be transformed physically from the austere woman we
have seen throughout the film to the warm Italian housewife.
Her rectangular glasses are gone, and her short, mannish
hairdo is covered by a cloth. The severe white blouses she
has worn throughout the film are replaced by the long black
dress of the Italian woman in the countryside. Even her pale
complexion is now replaced by a deep ruddy glow.

We are in the farmhouse of Guido's childhood memories
and it is filled with women. Guido has slipped deeper into
fantasy, and fills the farmhouse with a harem consisting of

all the women whom he knows or has known in the past. Guido enters and the women rush to greet him. Outside the door it is snowing. He begins to distribute gifts to the women. Luisa shows Guido a black girl she has brought for him. The girl dances to the tune of Saraghina's rhumba. Guido then is undressed and wrapped in a towel as he was when he was a boy. He is led to the huge barrel in which he bathed in wine lees as a boy. As he walks towards it he sees Rosella sitting on a balcony above him, reminding us of the little girl who invoked the words "ASA NISI MASA" in the farmhouse memory. She too sat on a balcony above the tub and tossed cherries down to the children bathing in it. Guido is surprised to see her and she likens herself to the talking cricket, the nagging conscience of Pinochio. A few moments later Rosella and an actress named Edy open a trap door above the bath and gaze down upon Guido. He is floating contentedly in the tub full of suds, with his hands crossed and flapping in a gesture identical to the one the girl of his childhood memory used when invoking the magic words, "ASA NISI MASA."

After he leaves the tub he lies on the floor where the women continue to wrap him in towels. Suddenly a commotion erupts and Jacqueline, an aged dancer, emerges from the basement in a hail of feathers. She is in full costume though clearly over the hill and out of shape. She protests the fact that she is to be sent upstairs to join the other women who have grown too old to please Guido. Guido maintains that it is the house rule, but she refuses to accept it. Suddenly, the French actress turns on Guido and says that "It's an absurd rule." Suddenly all the other women turn on him, and to the tune of the "Valkyrie" theme they commence to revolt against him. Guido picks up a whip and fights back. Throughout the chaos of the revolution, Luisa calmly tells Rosella that this happens almost every night. Eventually order is restored. The black girl jumps into place like a lion subdued by a lion tamer. All the women applaud Guido.

Jacqueline is allowed to perform her old dance once more, but her attempt is merely a ludicrous caricature of the past. Finally, followed still by the spotlight, she is led upstairs to the second floor and oblivion. Guido then gives a speech to the women seated at the dinner table, in which he says that happiness consists of being able to tell the truth without hurting anyone. For a moment we see Carla playing a harp in the foreground. A tear trickles down her cheek. Luisa then leaves the table. She fetches a bucket from the back of the room and begins to scrub the floor. "I didn't understand," she says contentedly, "this is how things should be. Do you see how good I am, Guido? What a fool I was. It took me twenty years to understand." Dissolve.

Scene 26: Close-up of Guido, his head bowed. He is sitting in a dim movie theater. His entourage is scattered throughout the theater. Behind him sits Daumier who pointedly

uotes from Stendahl to the effect that the self-centered man
ill end up by strangling upon his own emotions. Fed up with
aumier's ceaseless criticisms, Guido momentarily fantasizes
aumier's execution. He lifts his finger in a signal. Two
en approach Daumier and lead him from his seat. A hood is
laced over his head and he is summarily hung.

Guido's reverie is broken by Rosella, who asks whether
e is sitting near the door for a quick exit. Suddenly the
roducer enters the theater with Conocchia. The producer
arns Guido that the time has arrived to decide upon the
asting for the picture. He says that it has taken Guido so
ong that they are the joke of the industry. The lights dim
nd a picture flickers on the screen.

An actress enters through a door on the screen. She is
ressed in Carla's clothes and imitates her mannerisms. In
the audience Luisa smiles bitterly. Guido, on the other
and, hides his face in dismay. The producer asks how Guido
likes the actress, but he does not respond.

On the screen we see a new actress. She is thin with
sharply chiseled features, the same actress whose picture
Luisa spotted on her dresser while picking up a box of pills
after making her mysterious phone call (presumably to Enrico)
in the hotel room scene. On screen, Guido tells the actress
that she is to play a defeated woman with no fight left in
her. The actress, in close-up, reads the lines, "I'm offering you your freedom. You don't need me anymore. I'm only

in your way."

Tina, Enrico's friend, asks who the actress is portraying and Luisa answers, "Can't you guess? It's the wife." On screen the actress says angrily, "I don't care what you do, just be honest about this." In the audience Guido, attempting to apologize to Luisa for his depiction of her on the screen, quietly says, "Luisa, I love you." On screen the actress seems to answer him. As the film cuts from Guido's apology to her face, she says bitterly, "You lie with every breath." On screen, Guido, coaching the actress, asks her to repeat the line and she does. On screen, Guido then tells her to put on a pair of glasses. They are exactly like Luisa's. He tells her that the actor will ask her if she wants a separation and what will she do alone. She is to answer, "Aren't I alone now?"

In the audience the producer shouts, "Guido, you shouldn't think twice. This one is perfect." Another actress appears on the screen as Carla. Luisa, in the audience, takes her glasses off, perhaps in reaction to the actress' appearance on the screen, and yawns. We then see her walking up the theater stairs past Guido, and leaving through the door. He pauses for a moment and then follows her. In the hallway they confront each other. Luisa says that his film is a lie. Seated on the edge of a stairway, Guido sadly says that he is not going to make the film. Luisa ignores his capitulation. Angrily she screams, "What can you teach other people? You're not even honest with the woman who shares your life." Finally she says, "We had to come to a final decision. Well, my mind's made up now. You can go to Hell!" She then walks out on him and leaves him sitting in the shadows of the hall.

Guido returns to the theater. In the distance we hear the Saraghina rhumba. On screen, a huge woman, testing for the part of Saraghina runs around in circles. A boy dressed in the school uniform watches her. Guido turns away from the screen. In the audience Conocchia presents the producer with a new set of cost figures. We cut to a shot of another actress testing for the part of Saraghina as the producer says, "I'm not paying this, Conocchia. You've gone crazy." On screen we hear the voice of a small boy saying, "Saraghina, look. We have money."

On the screen a succession of actresses appear playing the part of Carla on the telephone. She asks not to be left alone. Guido, in the audience, covers his face with his hands. On screen, a huge fan swoops down towards the camera. We see Guido berating an actor dressed as a bishop or Cardinal. A fat actress playing the part of Carla laughs. The Cardinal swivels on a revolving platform. We see another Saraghina and then a close-up of a Carla while a boy shouts, "Money, Saraghina, money." The Cardinal swivels on the platform. The huge feathered fan is pulled back. The succession of images on the screen has turned into a kind of phantasmagoria.

The producer demands an opinion. Two men approach Guido
on either side. It is Claudia's manager along with the other
man whom we saw in the opening dream sequence, the one who
pulled Guido down from the sky. The second man introduces
himself as Claudia's press agent. He says that he met Guido
fifteen years ago and asks him if he remembers. Guido nods
yes, a rather ironic answer since the man has appeared in
Guido's dreams. He tells Guido that Claudia has arrived.

At the top of the stairs, against the doorway, we see
Claudia, the real actress rather than the muse, silhouetted.
She is dressed in black, with feathers, unlike the muse who
is always dressed in white. Guido rushes to meet her. They
leave the theater together, walking downstairs to her car.
Then they drive away from the theater.

Inside the car, Guido asks Claudia about the men in her
life. He asks her whom she loves and she answers, laughing-
ly, "You." She asks about the picture, but Guido, without
answering her question, asks her if she could walk out on
everything and start all over again. He asks if she could be
faithful to one single thing. He says, "Suppose I told you,
Claudia . . . ," but before he can finish what appears to be
a confession of his love she asks, "Where are we going? I
don't know the way." Then without answering his earlier
question she asks him if he could be faithful. Once again
Guido does not answer her but, rather, tells her that the

springs are nearby and that she should turn soon. Then,
without answering her question directly he says "No, the
character I'm thinking of couldn't. He wants to possess and
devour everything." Then he tells her that this character
meets a girl at the springs who gives him water to heal him.
"It is obvious that she could be his salvation," Guido says.
He adds, "You'll wear white with long hair just as you have
now."

The camera pans across a small, ancient town square as
the headlights of the car sweep across it. The camera pans
up to a brightly lit window in one of the ancient walls of
the buildings. Guido imagines that he sees Claudia, the
muse, dressed in white and standing in a white room within
the window. We see Claudia leave the room carrying an oil
lamp. A moment later she leaves the building and walks toward a table which has appeared, in Guido's imagination, in
the center of the plaza. Claudia places the lamp upon the
table. She then circles the table, first to the left and
then to the right. Then, both she and the table vanish as
Guido's reverie ends.

We see Claudia profiled in the car. "And then what?"
she asks. Claudia and Guido get out of the car and walk into
the courtyard. Claudia tells him that she hasn't much sympa-
thy for the man he has described as the protagonist of his
film. Guido, progressively becoming more disillusioned with
the fact that the real Claudia doesn't measure up to the

figure in his fantasies, lashes out at her, "What a pest you are, just like all the others." Claudia in turn tells him that he dresses like an old man. She says that she can't understand why the man in the film rejects a girl who can be his salvation. Guido answers that the man rejects her because he doesn't believe it but Claudia responds, "Because he doesn't know how to love." Guido answers, "Because no woman can change a man." Claudia repeats, "Because he doesn't know how to love." "And because I don't want to film another lie," says Guido. "He doesn't know how to love," answers Claudia. Guido then apologizes for bringing her to the spa. "You swindler," she says, "so there's no part for me in the film?" Guido answers, ". . . There's not even a film. There's nothing, nothing at all."

Claudia's face, in close-up, is suddenly washed out by the glare of automobile headlights. A group of cars pull up to the piazza, carrying many in Guido's entourage, including Claudia's press agent, Conocchia, and the producer. There is going to be a cocktail party for the press the next day at the spaceship to kick off the production of the film. The camera zooms in on Guido's face, as he shields it from the glare of the headlights. "Guido," his producer shouts, "we're finally in business."

Scene 27: In contrast to the darkness of the piazza at night, the screen is now filled with sunlight. We see the rear of a black car with three men in the back seat moving away from the camera. The man in the middle is Guido. The car is in the center now of many rows of cars, all moving towards the launching tower in the distance. The shot is a reprise of the first shot of the film, in which Guido's car, moving away from the camera, is trapped among many rows of cars in a traffic jam in an underground tunnel. This similarity of shots is just one of many indications, such as the change in lighting, that we have once again moved inside Guido's head. Unlike the tunnel sequence, however, the cars here rapidly pull away from the camera. The pace of this entire scene, in fact, is swift, if not frantic. Guido projects all of his hidden and repressed fears of facing up to the hopelessness of his situation into a fantasy of the upcoming press conference, triggered by the producer's announcement that he has invited the press to a cocktail party at the spaceship the next day. In the ensuing scene, Guido conjures up in his thoughts a phantasmagorical vision of the press conference as a kind of last judgment, a final reckoning in which his various inadequacies are exposed to public ridicule.

In the second shot of the scene we see that the cars are now parked, and that Guido is now being guided from the parking lot to the press conference by two of his assistants. At one point he attempts to go limp and sit on the ground, but the assistants, one on each arm, hold him up and prevail upon him to walk towards the conference. Once Guido nears the

launching tower he is beseiged by groups of reporters. They
attempt to question him while he tries to elude them. As he
continues to approach the tower he passes Maurice and Maya.
Maurice waves, crosses both fingers, and wishes him good
luck. The pace of the editing, in conjunction with that of
the background music and the movement of the actors within
the frame, is rather swift.

Guido approaches the stage and the producer says to him,
"We've been waiting for you for three days. It's winter already." Once again, the surrealistic nature of the scene as
a fantasy unfolding within Guido's mind is implicit in the
producer's statement and in the sudden transition from the
oppressively warm summer sun which bathes the garden of the
spa to the cold winter light which pervades this scene. The
breeze of the summer night which blows through the piazza is
intensified by Guido's imagination, as he stands there imagining this press conference, into the roaring wind which
whips out of the sea preceding the blasts of winter.

The camera travels right, past a long line of reporters
poised on the edges of their chairs shouting questions at
Guido. At the stage Guido looks like he is in a state of
near collapse as the producer, Claudia's agents, and others
prod him to answer the questions of the reporters. Finally
the newsmen rush the stage as their questions turn more hostile. "You has-been," one of them shouts, "How could your
own life interest the public?" Guido ducks behind the table

ut his producer and Conocchia pull him back up. An American
ady reporter turns to the camera and triumphantly declares
n English, "He's lost. He has nothing to say!" She laughs
n derision.

The producer continues to urge Guido to say something.
uido looks down at the surface of the table behind which he
s sitting. It is a mirror, and he sees the producer stand-
ng above him as he pleads, "Do it for me."* Some of the
eporters climb the stage. The camera pans the sea of hos-
ile faces below in front of the stage. Guido, in despera-
ion, calls out to Claudia and Rosella's spirits. He apolo-
izes to Conocchia for his treatment of him. The producer
ooks down towards Guido and tells him, "Make this picture or
'll ruin you." In the mirrored surface of the table we see
he reflection of Luisa, dressed in a wedding gown, in the
idst of the reporters in front of the stage.** "Won't you
e my husband any more?" she asks, "When will you truly marry
e?" Guido's reply is a complete <u>non sequitur</u>, as if he does
ot hear her correctly. He asks her if she really wants a
separation. Even here there is no communication between
them. Luisa answers, "I can't go on like this." We cut to a
shot of Luisa in the crowd. The camera pulls back from her

*From the point of view of the audience, which is the
point of view of the shot, the producer is upside down in the
mirror.

**From Guido's point of view, which is the point of view
of the shot, Luisa's face is reflected upside-down in the
mirror.

rapidly as newsmen swarm in front of her. She disappears in the crowd.

Guido sits down again. They try to get him to stand but he refuses. Bruno, one of his assistants, bends down beside him and whispers in his ear, "It's in your right hand pocket. Suddenly Guido sheds his cloak and ducks underneath the table As he crawls underneath the table towards the camera, the reporters continue to shout questions at him as they stick their heads under the table. Guido answers, "One minute. I'm thinking of what I should say." Guido crawls forward away from this group of reporters and then pauses. Behind him, the threatening, distorted shadows of heads and hands loom up against the table cloth which is draped over this part of the table. He lies on his side and withdraws a gun from his pocket. He puts the gun to his head.

The film cuts to a shot of Guido's mother, her arms spread in fear. She runs forward. The camera swiftly zooms away from her, as she stands helplessly upon the beach. "Where are you running to, you wretched boy?" she cries, as she fades into the background. Here we have a kind of fantasy within a fantasy. As Guido fantasizes his suicide at the imaginary press conference, he also pictures himself, within the fantasy, conjuring up a final image of his mother as he prepares to kill himself.

The film cuts to a close-up of the back of Guido's head, which recoils as the gunshot explodes. His head then sinks to the ground.

Scene 28: A shot of one of the launching towers from below.
The wind blows and streamers on the tower flap in the breeze.
The camera pans left to a second tower, and the view is identical to that which we had of the tower while Guido was soaring through the clouds in the opening fantasy of the film.

The film cuts to a long shot of a group of people standing beneath the towers. Among them is Guido. Guido tells
the workers to take everything down. We have now returned to
the real world. Guido, as he has previously told both his
wife and Claudia, has finally admitted that he cannot make
the film. Certainly the phantasmagoria which, as we have
seen, races through his mind when his producer announces the
press conference has served to confirm his decision not to
proceed with the film.

Daumier, who has been observing Guido, tells him that he
did the right thing. As they enter Guido's car, Daumier begins one of his nonstop monologues, commending Guido for his
decision to scrap the film while, in the process, damning him
with faint praise. "The world abounds with superfluity," he
says, "Why add disorder to disorder? . . . It's better to
destroy than to create what is unessential." From the car
Guido gazes up at the tower. A section of the superstructure
tumbles heavily to the ground. Ironically Daumier continues,
"We're already suffocated by words, by sounds and images that

have no reason to exist. . . . Any man worthy to be called an artist should swear one oath, dedication to silence."

While Daumier continues to speak, the camera zooms to a close-up of Guido, who drifts off, once more, into fantasy. Suddenly he imagines that Maurice approaches the car. He looks in on Daumier's side of the car and announces, "We're ready to begin." He then runs to Guido's, the driver's side, and says, "All my best wishes." He then waves his right arm as if gesturing for the show to begin. We see the back of Claudia's head. She turns toward the camera. As Guido's ideal woman, she is once again dressed in her white nurse's costume. Guido touches the bridge of his nose. We see the nurses from the farmhouse, dressed in white and holding Guido, the young child, as they stand upon the sand. We then see Saraghina, her hands upon her hips, also dressed in white in Guido's imagination. Then we see Guido's parents dressed in white.

In the car, Daumier continues his monologue, but now his face is obscured by the reflection of the sky upon the windshield. In Guido's imagination, Claudia smiles and turns to the left. The camera pans left as she begins walking off toward the left of the frame. Then we see Carla dressed in white, with the Cardinal and the other clerics in the background. While we hear Daumier saying, "Why piece together the tatters of your life?" Carla and the clerics begin walking towards the right of the screen as the camera pans right with

them. This is followed by a long shot encompassing even a
larger number of people drawn from Guido's life, including
nurses and clerics, all walking toward the right. Their
movement, which we shall discover is toward Guido and the
towers, is dramatically contrasted with that of Claudia, who
walked toward the left and, apparently, out of Guido's life
and consciousness.

This sequence is followed by a close-up of Guido in the
car. We hear his interior voice on the sound track as he
meditates upon his condition. He experiences a new sense of
joy and renewal. The film cuts to a shot of Luisa and
Rosella, dressed in white, walking inside the circus ring.
"Forgive me, sweet creatures," are the words of Guido's
interior voice as he fantasizes the presence of the two women.
"I didn't understand. I didn't know." Luisa walks toward
the camera while Rosella stops and then walks toward the
background and finally out of view. "I do accept you, I do
love you. . . . How simple it is. . . . Luisa, I've been
freed," are the words in Guido's mind. Suddenly everything
seems meaningful to Guido, a feeling which he says he can't
explain. We see Maurice running across the circus ring as
spotlights turn on. The lighting of this sequence has been
considerably dimmer than that of the press conference fantasy,
and now it is clear that day is quickly passing into night.
It is the hour of dusk. Guido admits to himself, for the
first time, "All the confusion of my life has been a
reflection of myself."

We see Luisa in close-up. We hear Guido's interior
voice, "Life is a holiday. Let us live it together." Luisa
remains expressionless. He continues, "That's all I can say,
Luisa--to you and the others. Accept me as I am. Only then
will we discover each other." Luisa smiles and answers, "I'm
not sure that's true. But I can try, if you'll help me." In
the background we begin to hear music. A band of four clowns
playing various instruments marches across the screen followed
by Guido as a schoolboy. He is in his uniform, but now the
uniform is white. He is playing a flute.

Now all the people from Guido's life, whom we have earlier seen marching to the right, such as Carla, the prelates,
and Guido's parents, enter the circus ring as Maurice wel-
comes them back. Guido enters the ring and begins to direct
the other people. He shows the band where to march and then
whispers in the boy's ear. The band circles a large podium
where a full-scale orchestra now plays. They then line up
perpendicular to a large curtain. The boy marches to the
right of the curtain playing his flute. The curtain opens
and, behind it, a large mass of people begins to descend the
stairs which lead to the tower. The music intensifies.
These people, dressed in their regular clothes, are generally
figures who have played a secondary role in Guido's life. We
see, for instance, the producer talking to his assistants as
they walk down the stairway.

Guido, bullhorn in hand, attempts to organize the people

in the center of the ring. He stops and kneels before the Cardinal. In the background, a few of the people, having mounted the rim of the circus ring, begin to dance tentatively in a clockwise direction. The prelates go to join them. Guido waves to his parents as they go to join the people on the rim who have now begun to dance in place, as if they were awaiting direction. Carla approaches Guido and tells him that she understands that he is trying to tell everybody that he can't do without them. Guido promises to call her the next day and then tells her to join the others. Maurice grabs her arm and leads her to the circle. Guido, shouting through his bullhorn, directs the people around the circle. He tells them to spread out and to hold hands. Guido drops both his hands as a signal and there is a fanfare, followed by a more intense rendition of the musical theme. Maurice raises his cane as another signal. He begins leading the long chain of people standing on the rim of the circle in a counter-clockwise dance. Guido, still in the center of the ring, walks to the right, where Luisa is standing. He takes her hand. She pauses for a moment, seemingly hesitant, and then smiles and follows Guido as he leads her to the rim of the circle where the people are dancing. Luisa and Guido mount the rim of the middle of the human chain. They join hands with those next to them and become part of the circle of dancers. The dance continues.

In the next cut it is nighttime. The camera is outside

the circle, lit by spotlights, as the last two dancers dance
off to the right. In the background we see the band of
clowns with the young Guido in the circus ring. The band
marches back and forth and finally leaves the ring. Guido,
the schoolboy, is alone in the spotlight. As he begins to
march out of the circle, following the clowns, the footlights
around the rim of the circle begin to go out. With the spotlight following him in the darkness, the child, still playing
the flute, marches out of the ring and the picture. The last
few footlights fade and the screen is dark.

APPENDIX B

THE PINOCCHIO MOTIF IN <u>8-1/2</u>

Besides constituting a movement towards psychic wholeness, the individuation process is also one of growth and
development. Fellini employs a rather subtle and understated
motif drawn from Italian literature to indicate that Guido is
undergoing this process. The film is studded with references
to the tale of Pinocchio. Most of these references are quite
subtle, but at least one is completely explicit. To understand the nature of these references, however, a brief summary of the story might be helpful.

<u>The Adventures of Pinocchio</u> was written in 1883 by Carlo
Lorenzini under the pen name of C. Collodi. Originally the
tale was presented in a serialized form in an Italian maga-
zine of the times. Although generally regarded today as a
children's story, it was written to satirize, in the manner
of a children's tale, the political and social corruption of
the times. Various prominent Italians were thus caricatured
in the form of the various creatures whom Pinocchio meets in
the course of his adventures.

Briefly, the story follows the adventures of a wooden
puppet named Pinocchio, carved from a piece of wood that
talks by a carver named Gepetto. Unlike the romanticized
Disney version of the character, Pinocchio, in the story, is

224

totally devoid of any human feelings. He is an evil and
repulsive little creature who destroys all those who attempt
to help him and is easily drawn to bad companions. As soon
as Gepetto carves his legs, Pinocchio kicks him. Ultimately
Gepetto is thrown in prison due to Pinocchio's antics, and
when Pinocchio returns home and is rebuked by the Talking
Cricket, representative of his conscience and portrayed in
the syrupy Disney version as Jimminy Cricket, he promptly
flattens the cricket against the wall with a hammer. A
series of misadventures follow in which Pinocchio's lack of
humanity and feelings leads to a series of disasters from
which he only narrowly escapes. At times, he survives only
due to the machinations of the Fairy with Blue Hair, who becomes his guardian angel. She also begins to imbue him with
a sense of morality. The most famous example of this, and
one which has some bearing on 8-1/2, occurs when she punishes
him for his inability to tell the truth by causing his nose
to grow longer every time he tells a lie.

Eventually, after a long series of misadventures, Pinocchio does begin to develop some sense of humanity, reflected
in a growing concern for the welfare of others. This new
concern culminates in his rescue of Gepetto from the bowels
of a giant fish. As his character begins to develop towards
a greater sense of humanity, Pinocchio begins to wish that he
were a real little boy. A conversation ensues between him
and the Fairy with Blue Hair which has, perhaps, at least an

allegorical relationship to the themes of 8-1/2:

> '. . . I always remain no bigger than a ninepin.'
> 'But you cannot grow,' replied the Fairy.
> 'Why?'
> 'Because puppets never grow. They are born
> puppets, live puppets, and die puppets.'
> 'Oh I am sick of being a puppet,' cried Pinocchio,
> giving himself a slap. 'It is time that I became a
> man.'
> 'And you will become one, if you know how to
> deserve it.'
> 'Not really? And what can I do to deserve it?'
> 'A very easy thing, by learning to be a good boy.'[1]

For Pinocchio, learning to be a good boy means learning to be
concerned with the needs of others, learning to give as well
as to receive. At the end of the story, of course, he meets
the test by rescuing Gepetto and is rewarded by being transformed by the Fairy with Blue Hair into a real little boy.

The most obvious parallel between this story and 8-1/2
is that both works are essentially about personal development. Both Pinocchio and Guido must learn to relate to the
needs and desires of others. Pinocchio's lack of humanity,
of course, is embodied in the fact that he is literally a
wooden boy, a puppet. His transformation, therefore, is literal as well as figurative. When he learns to act like a
human being he literally becomes one. Moreover, Pinocchio's
development is guided by a figure resembling the anima,
namely the Fairy with Blue Hair.

Thus, there are obvious resemblances between the story
of Pinocchio and the individuation process, and in this

---

[1] C. Collodi, The Adventures of Pinocchio (New York,
1946), p. 146.

respect the tale reminds us of 8-1/2. The fact that both works are stories of self-realization, however, is scarcely a significant basis of comparison in itself. After all, there are countless works, both in literature and film, about self-realization. There is, however, a consistent pattern of references, both in terms of gestures and dialogue in 8-1/2 which point unmistakably to Pinocchio as a literary precursor of the film.

There is a consistent pattern of gestures on the part of Guido, for instance, in which he taps or rubs his nose, usually in conjunction with one of his falsehoods or with one of his fantasies. Occasionally this gesture takes the form of Guido pulling his glasses down his nose. When Guido first experiences the vision of Claudia at the spa, for instance, he pulls his glasses down the bridge of his nose. Then, as he watches her glide into the spa, he taps his nose with his finger. Later, at the night club, when Carla waves covertly to Guido, he covers his nose with his hand. When Guido, during his audience with the Cardinal, spots the fat lady who reminds him of Saraghina walking down the hill, he pulls his glasses down his nose and lapses into the Saraghina fantasy. At the end of the film, when Guido envisions Claudia while sitting in his car on the beach, he touches the top of his nose over his glasses. So far, Guido's tendency to touch his nose can be seen as a prelude to his fantasies. In one case it is associated with his illicit relationship with Carla.

The relationship of this gesture to the Pinocchio tale
will be more evident, however, if we look at two other examples. The first occurs at the cafe after Luisa spots Carla
and begins to berate Guido about her presence. Luisa is denouncing Guido angrily because he has lied to her about his
activities at the spa. He denies that he even knew that Carla
was there and she replies, "He can drive you out of your
mind. He talks exactly as if he were telling the truth."
She continues, "How can you live like this? You lie so well
I can't tell true from false. Is it possible you don't know
the difference? . . ." Throughout this entire polemic, Guido
characteristically strokes his nose as he listens. Then as
she continues her diatribe with lines like, "It's humiliating
to have to act like a scandalized housewife," Guido momentarily covers his nose with his hand and then begins to tap the
tip of his nose with his finger.

Here Guido's nose tapping is juxtaposed directly to
Luisa's accusation that he has lied to her. We then recall
that Pinocchio's nose grew longer every time he told a lie.
Guido covers his nose when he sees Carla at the night club,
and this too is related to his deception and betrayal of
Luisa. Often Guido toys with his nose as a prelude to one of
his fantasies, and these imaginary episodes are also, in a
sense, falsifications of reality. It is almost, at times, as
if Guido were absentmindedly testing the size of his own
nose.

The most direct parallel, in this regard, between 8-1/2 and Pinocchio can be found early in the night club scene. As Mezzabotta and Gloria dance, the film cuts to a close-up of Guido. He is wearing an elongated false nose made of dough which he taps with his fingers. Here Guido's nose has literally grown longer and once more we are reminded of Pinocchio. The open and honest nature of Mezzabotta's relationship with Gloria is contrasted in the scene with the secretive and illicit quality of Guido's affair with Carla. While Mezzabotta openly flaunts his engagement to Gloria, Guido's affair is apparently known to only one other person in the scene, and he goes to great pains to maintain this secrecy. Once again we are reminded of Pinocchio.

The motif of offering water is an important one in the film, and is associated with Guido's anima projection. At the fountain of the spa Guido imagines that Claudia offers him a glass of water. In his film, the protagonist is offered a glass of water by the woman who can be his salvation, also played by Claudia. In Pinocchio one of the Blue-Haired Fairy's incarnations is a woman who offers water to Pinocchio, whom she finds along a road desperately begging food and water from those passing by. The scene is an important one in the book, for it ultimately leads to the first step in Pinocchio's salvation, and thus the parallel to 8-1/2 is rather striking. The sea, as well, is an important motif in Pinocchio just as it is in the film.

Like Guido, Pinocchio falls in with bad companions at school. He gets into serious difficulties when he runs away from school with them. The circus plays an important role in Pinocchio, and it is the central motif of the concluding scene of 8-1'2, which takes place in a circus ring.

The most explicit reference to Pinocchio, however, occurs during the harem fantasy. As Guido is about to enter his bath, he notices Rosella perched on a balcony above him. Sitting over the edge of the balcony, she reminds us of the young girl who sat on the edge of the trap door and threw cherries down at the boys in the bath of wine lees. "You're here too, Rosella?" Guido exclaims. "Yes, like Pinocchio's nagging conscience," she answers. Implicitly she identifies herself with the cricket who serves as Pinocchio's conscience in the book.

In many respects she is like the Talking Cricket in Pinocchio. In the story, the cricket is a rather supernatural figure, and Rosella dabbles in the occult and is in touch with the spirit world. Just as Pinocchio eventually turns to the cricket for advice, so Guido looks to Rosella and her spirits for advice. At the launching tower, when he discusses his marriage with her, he asks what advice her spirits have for him. She answers that the spirits always say the same thing for they know him well. They say that he is free, but that he must choose and he doesn't have much time left. Later, in his press conference fantasy, at the height of his

difficulties, he cries to her for help. "Where are your
spirits now, Rosella?" he asks.

In the harem fantasy, her role is particularly reminiscent of the Talking Cricket whose warnings of danger are
never taken seriously by Pinocchio until it is too late. In
the story, Pinocchio is constantly being lured into situa-
tions which promise to fulfill his dream of a life without
work only to discover the dream turns into a nightmare. In
the seemingly Utopian land of Cocaigne, for instance, little
boys turn into jackasses. If, of course, he had heeded the
warnings of the Talking Cricket, he might have been spared
much hardship. Similarly, Guido's harem dissolves, at least
for a few moments, into rebellion. Rosella, however, provides him with a veiled warning of things to come, but Guido
is too complacent to perceive the nature of her statement.
"So you finally got your harem," she says as he is about to
enter his bath. "Tell me," she asks, "aren't you a little
afraid?" "Of what?" answers Guido, "Everything's perfect."
Rosella continues to play the role of the omniscient Cricket.
"Can I stay?" she asks, "I want to observe you." "As long as
you observe the house rules," Guido replies. Like Pinocchio,
of course, Guido is too complacent and self-confident to see
the possibility of danger ahead. Rosella's implicit suggestion that there is something he should be afraid of passes
unheeded.

Thus, it would seem that 8-1/2 is pervaded with numerous

references to <u>The Adventures of Pinocchio.</u> Guido's role in
the film is meant to be seen as analagous to Pinocchio's in
the story. Both are tales of self-realization which suggest
that one's humanity is contingent upon his willingness to
give as well as to receive love. Pinocchio is literally a
little wooden boy who realizes his potential for humanity
only after he learns this. Fellini suggests that Guido, like
Pinocchio, is also a kind of wooden boy. In the terms of
this analogy, he too must learn how to extend love to others
before he can develop fully as a human being and, in the
process, overcome his emotional and artistic paralysis.
Other characters in the film are also paralleled in the
story. Rosella, like Pinocchio's Talking Cricket, is explicitly portrayed in the film as Guido's conscience. Claudia,
like the Fairy with Blue Hair, serves as Guido's moral guide,
and, just as the Fairy teaches Pinocchio that he must be concerned with the well being of others, she teaches Guido that
he must know how to love. Just as Pinocchio is transformed
into a real little boy at the end of his story, so Guido,
having fantasized the death of his old self, begins to
develop towards a new humanity at the end of <u>8-1/2</u>.

BIBLIOGRAPHY

Antonioni, Michelangelo. "A Talk with Michelangelo Antonioni on His Work, . . ." L'Aventurra. New York: Grove Press, 1969.

Arnheim, Rudolf. Film as Art. Berkeley: University of California Press, 1957.

_____. Visual Thinking. Berkeley: University of California Press, 1969.

Bachman, Gideon. "Interview with Federico Fellini," Cinéma [Paris], 99 (1965), 71-89.

_____. "Interview with Federico Fellini," Sight and Sound, Spring 1964, pp. 82-84.

Barzini, Luigi. The Italians. New York: Bantam, 1964.

Bazin, Andre. What is Cinema? Trans. Hugh Gray. Berkeley: University of California Press, 1967.

Bergson, Henri. Duration and Simultaneity, trans. Leon Jacobson. New York: Bobbs-Merrill, 1962.

Bluestone, George. Novels into Film. Berkeley: University of California Press, 1957.

Bobker, Lee R. Elements of Film. New York: Harcourt, Brace, and World, 1969.

Boyer, Deena. The Two Hundred Days of 8-1/2, trans. Charles Ian Markman. New York: MacMillan, 1964.

Brooks, Cleanth. The Well Wrought Urn: Studies in the Structure of Poetry. New York: Harcourt, Brace, and World, 1947.

Budgen, Suzanne. Fellini. England: British Film Institute Education Department, 1966.

Callenbach, Ernest. "Acting, Being, and the Death of the Movie Aesthetic," New American Review, 8 (1970), 94-112.

Carson, L. M. Kit. David Holzman's Diary. New York: Farrar, Strauss, and Giroux, 1970.

Casty, Alan. The Dramatic Art of the Film. New York: Harper and Row, 1970.

Collodi, C. (Carlo Lorenzini). The Adventures of Pinocchio, trans. M. A. Murray. New York: Grosset and Dunlap, 1946.

de Laurot, Edouard. "La Strada--A Poem on Saintly Folly," Renaissance of the Film, ed. Julius Bellone. New York: MacMillan, 1970, pp. 264-276.

Dillard, R. H. W. "If We Were All Devils," Contempora, 1, No. 5 (January/April 1971), pp. 26-33.

Dumont, Dr. Mathew. The Absurd Healer. New York: Science House, 1968, pp. 96-101.

Durgnat, Raymond. Films and Feelings. Cambridge, Massachusetts: M.I.T. Press, 1967.

"8-1/2," Études Cinématographiques, 28-29 (Winter 1963).

Favazza, Armando. "Fellini: Analyst Without Portfolio," Man and the Movies, ed. W. R. Robinson. Baltimore: Penguin Books, 1967, pp. 180-190.

Fellini, Federico. "End of the Sweet Parade," Esquire, January 1963, pp. 98-108, 128, 130.

_____. 8-1/2 (subtitled). White Plains: Audio-Brandon, 1962.

_____. "Federico Fellini," Discussion, No. 1: American Film Institute, 1970.

_____. Fellini's Satyricon, ed. Dario Zanelli, trans. Eugene Walter and John Matthews. New York: Ballantine Books, 1969.

_____. "Huit et Demi," L'Avant-Scène du Cinéma. No. 63.

_____. Juliet of the Spirits (including "The Long Interview"), ed. Tullio Kezich, trans. Howard Greenfeld. New York: Ballantine Books, 1965.

_____. "The Road Beyond Neorealism," Film: A Montage of Theories, ed. Richard Dyer McCann. New York: E. P. Dutton and Company, 1966.

Fraisse, Paul. The Psychology of Time, trans. Jennifer Leith. New York: Harper and Row, 1963.

Freud, Sigmund. Character and Culture. New York: Collier Books, 1963.

_____. A General Introduction to Psychoanalysis, trans. Joan Riviere. New York: Washington Square Press, 1924.

Freud, Sigmund. The Interpretation of Dreams, ed. and trans.
James Strachey. New York: Avon, 1900.

Gessner, Robert. The Moving Image: A Guide to Cinema Lit-
eracy. New York: E. P. Dutton and Company, 1970.

Gilliatt, Penelope. "Review of 8-1/2," Observer London, 25
August 1963.

Gruen, John. "Interview with Fellini," New York Herald
Tribune, 1 August 1965, p. 33.

Harcourt, Peter. "The Secret Life of Federico Fellini," Film
Quarterly, 19 (Spring 1966), 4-19.

Heidegger, Martin. "What is Metaphysics?" Existence and
Being, trans. by R. F. C. Hull and Alan Crick. Chicago:
Henry Regnery Company, 1949, pp. 325-361.

Holland, Norman. "The Follies of Fellini," Renaissance of
the Film, ed. Julius Bellone. New York: MacMillan,
1970, pp. 79-90.

Hughes, Eileen Lanouette. On the Set of Fellini Satyricon.
New York: William Morrow and Company, 1971.

Huss, Roy, and Norman Silverstein. The Film Experience. New
York: Dell Publishing Company, 1958.

Jacobs, Lewis, ed. The Movies as Medium. New York: Farrar,
Strauss, and Giroux, 1970.

Jung, C. G. The Archetypes and the Collective Unconscious,
Collected Works, Volume 9, Part I, trans. R. F. C. Hull.
Princeton: Princeton University Press, 1959.

_____. Flying Saucers: A Modern Myth of Things Seen in
the Sky, trans. R. F. C. Hull. New York: New American
Library, 1959.

_____. Four Archetypes: Mother, Rebirth, Spirit, Trick-
ster, from Collected Works, Volume 9, Part I, trans.
R. F. C. Hull. Princeton: Princeton University Press,
1959.

_____, ed. Man and His Symbols. New York: Dell Publishing
Company, 1964.

_____. Memories, Dreams, Refelctions, ed. Aniela Jaffé,
trans. Richard and Clara Winston. New York: Vintage
Books, 1961.

Jung, Carl G. Modern Man in Search of a Soul, trans. C. F. Barnes and Stanley Dell. New York: Harcourt, Brace and World, 1933.

_____. Psyche and Symbol, ed. Violet S. de Laszlo. Garden City: Doubleday Anchor Books, 1958.

_____. Psychology and Religion. New Haven: Yale University Press, 1938.

_____. The Psychology of Transference, Collected Works, Volume 16, trans. R. F. C. Hull. Princeton: Princeton University Press, 1954.

_____. Symbols of Transformation, trans. R. F. C. Hull, 2 vols. New York: Harper and Brothers, 1952.

_____. Two Essays on Analytical Psychology, trans. R. F. C. Hull. New York: World Publishing Company, 1953.

Kauffman, Stanley. A World on Film. New York: Harper and Row, 1958.

Kinder, Marsha, and Beverle Houston. Close-up: A Critical Perspective on Film. New York: Harcourt, Brace, Jovanovich, 1972.

Kracauer, Siegfried. Theory of Film: The Redemption of Physical Reality. New York: Oxford University Press, 1960.

Lawson, John Howard. Film: The Creative Process. New York: Hill and Wang, 1964.

Levine, Irving. "'I Was Born for the Cinema' A Conversation with Federico Fellini," Film Comment, 4 (Fall 1966), 80-83.

McDonald, Dwight. "8-1/2 Fellini's Obvious Masterpiece," On Movies. New Jersey: Prentice-Hall, 1969, pp. 15-31.

Merleau-Ponty, "Le Cinéma et la Nouvelle Psychologie," Sens et non sens. Paris: Nagel, 1948.

Metz, Christian. "La Construction 'en abyme' dans Huit et Demi de Fellini," Essais sur la Signification au Cinéma. Paris: Editions Klincksieck, 1968, pp. 223-228.

Paolucci, Anne. "Italian Film: Antonioni, Fellini, Bolognini," Massachusetts Review, 12 (Summer 1966), 556-567.

Pechter, William S. Twenty-four Times a Second. New York: Harper and Row, 1960.

Peri, Renzo. "Federico Fellini: An Interview," Film Quarterly, 15 (Fall 1961), 30-33.

Perry, Ted. "A Contextual Study of M. Antonioni's Film L'Eclisse," Speech Monographs, 37 (June 1970), 79-100.

_____. "Signifiers in Fellini's 8-1/2," Forum Italicum, 6, No. 1 (March 1972), 79-86.

Priestly, J. B. Man and Time. New York: Dell Publishing Company, 1964.

Reisz, Karel, and Gavin Miller. The Technique of Film Editing. New York: Hastings House, 1953.

Rhode, Eric. "Film Review--8-1/2," Sight and Sound, Autumn 1963, p. 193.

Richardson, Robert. Literature and Film. Bloomington: Indiana University Press, 1969.

Ross, Lillian. "10-1/2," The New Yorker, 30 October 1963, pp. 63-107.

Salachas, Gilbert. Federico Fellini: An Investigation into His Films and Philosophy, trans. Rosalie Siegel. New York: Crown Publishers, 1963.

Sartre, Jean-Paul. Being and Nothingness: An Essay on Phenomenological Ontology, trans. Hazel E. Barnes. New York: Washington Square Press, 1953.

Schopenhauer, Arthur. The World as Will and Idea, trans. R. B. Haldane and J. Kemp. Garden City: Doubleday and Company, 1844.

Simon, John. "Fellini's 8-1/2¢ Fancy," Private Screenings. New York: MacMillan, 1967.

Solmi, Angelo. Fellini, trans. Elizabeth Greenwood. London: Merlin Press, 1967.

Taylor, John Russell. "Federico Fellini," Cinema Eye, Cinema Ear. New York: Hill and Wang, 1965, pp. 15-51.

Walter, Eugene. "The Wizardry of Fellini," Films and Filming, 12 (June 1966), 18-26.

Watts, Alan W. The Way of Zen. New York: New American
    Library, 1957.

Whitmont, Edward C. The Symbolic Quest. New York: G. P.
    Putnam's Sons, 1960.

The Arno Press Cinema Program

THE LITERATURE OF CINEMA

Series I & II

Agate, James. **Around Cinemas.** 1946.

Agate, James. **Around Cinemas.** (Second Series). 1948.

American Academy of Political and Social Science. **The Motion Picture in Its Economic and Social Aspects,** edited by Clyde L. King. **The Motion Picture Industry,** edited by Gordon S. Watkins. *The Annals,* November, 1926/1927.

L'Art Cinematographique, Nos. 1-8. 1926-1931.

Balcon, Michael, Ernest Lindgren, Forsyth Hardy and Roger Manvell. **Twenty Years of British Film, 1925-1945.** 1947.

Bardèche, Maurice and Robert Brasillach. **The History of Motion Pictures,** edited by Iris Barry. 1938.

Benoit-Levy, Jean. **The Art of the Motion Picture.** 1946.

Blumer, Herbert. **Movies and Conduct.** 1933.

Blumer, Herbert and Philip M. Hauser. **Movies, Delinquency, and Crime.** 1933.

Buckle, Gerard Fort. **The Mind and the Film.** 1926.

Carter, Huntly. **The New Spirit in the Cinema.** 1930.

Carter, Huntly. **The New Spirit in the Russian Theatre, 1917-1928.** 1929.

Carter, Huntly. **The New Theatre and Cinema of Soviet Russia.** 1924.

Charters, W. W. **Motion Pictures and Youth.** 1933.

Cinema Commission of Inquiry. **The Cinema: Its Present Position and Future Possibilities.** 1917.

Dale, Edgar. **Children's Attendance at Motion Pictures.** Dysinger, Wendell S. and Christian A. Ruckmick. **The Emotional Responses of Children to the Motion Picture Situation.** 1935.

Dale, Edgar. **The Content of Motion Pictures.** 1935.

Dale, Edgar. **How to Appreciate Motion Pictures.** 1937.

Dale, Edgar, Fannie W. Dunn, Charles F. Hoban, Jr., and Etta Schneider. **Motion Pictures in Education: A Summary of the Literature.** 1938.

Davy, Charles. **Footnotes to the Film.** 1938.

Dickinson, Thorold and Catherine De la Roche. **Soviet Cinema.** 1948.

Dickson, W. K. L., and Antonia Dickson. **History of the Kinetograph, Kinetoscope and Kinetophonograph.** 1895.

Forman, Henry James. Our Movie Made Children. 1935.

Freeburg, Victor Oscar. The Art of Photoplay Making. 1918.

Freeburg, Victor Oscar. Pictorial Beauty on the Screen. 1923.

Hall, Hal, editor. Cinematographic Annual, 2 vols. 1930/1931.

Hampton, Benjamiñ B. A History of the Movies. 1931.

Hardy, Forsyth. Scandinavian Film. 1952.

Hepworth, Cecil M. Animated Photography: The A B C of the Cinematograph. 1900.

Hoban, Charles F., Jr., and Edward B. Van Ormer. Instructional Film Research 1918-1950. 1950.

Holaday, Perry W. and George D. Stoddard. Getting Ideas from the Movies. 1933.

Hopwood, Henry V. Living Pictures. 1899.

Hulfish, David S. Motion-Picture Work. 1915.

Hunter, William. Scrutiny of Cinema. 1932.

Huntley, John. British Film Music. 1948.

Irwin, Will. The House That Shadows Built. 1928.

Jarratt, Vernon. The Italian Cinema. 1951.

Jenkins, C. Francis. Animated Pictures. 1898.

Lang, Edith and George West. Musical Accompaniment of Moving Pictures. 1920.

London, Kurt. Film Music. 1936.

Lutz, E [dwin] G [eorge]. The Motion-Picture Cameraman. 1927.

Manvell, Roger. Experiment in the Film. 1949.

Marey, Etienne Jules. Movement. 1895.

Martin, Olga J. Hollywood's Movie Commandments. 1937.

Mayer, J. P. Sociology of Film: Studies and Documents. 1946. New Introduction by J. P. Mayer.

Münsterberg, Hugo. The Photoplay: A Psychological Study. 1916.
Nicoll, Allardyce. Film and Theatre. 1936.

Noble, Peter. The Negro in Films. 1949.

Peters, Charles C. Motion Pictures and Standards of Morality. 1933.

Peterson, Ruth C. and L. L. Thurstone. Motion Pictures and the Social Attitudes of Children. Shuttleworth, Frank K. and Mark A. May. The Social Conduct and Attitudes of Movie Fans. 1933.

Phillips, Henry Albert. The Photodrama. 1914.

Photoplay Research Society. Opportunities in the Motion Picture Industry. 1922.

Rapée, Erno. Encyclopaedia of Music for Pictures. 1925.

Rapée, Erno. Motion Picture Moods for Pianists and Organists. 1924.

Renshaw, Samuel, Vernon L. Miller and Dorothy P. Marquis. Children's Sleep. 1933.

Rosten, Leo C. Hollywood: The Movie Colony, The Movie Makers. 1941.

Sadoul, Georges. French Film. 1953.

Screen Monographs I, 1923-1937. 1970.

Screen Monographs II, 1915-1930. 1970.

Sinclair, Upton. Upton Sinclair Presents William Fox. 1933.

Talbot, Frederick A. Moving Pictures. 1912.

Thorp, Margaret Farrand. America at the Movies. 1939.

Wollenberg, H. H. Fifty Years of German Film. 1948.

RELATED BOOKS AND PERIODICALS

Allister, Ray. Friese-Greene: Close-Up of an Inventor. 1948.

Art in Cinema: A Symposium of the Avant-Garde Film, edited by Frank Stauffacher. 1947.

The Art of Cinema: Selected Essays. New Foreword by George Amberg. 1971.

Balázs, Béla. Theory of the Film. 1952.

Barry, Iris. Let's Go to the Movies. 1926.

de Beauvoir, Simone. Brigitte Bardot and the Lolita Syndrome. 1960.

Carrick, Edward. Art and Design in the British Film. 1948.

Close Up. Vols. 1-10, 1927-1933 (all published).

Cogley, John. Report on Blacklisting. Part I: The Movies. 1956.

Eisenstein, S. M. Que Viva Mexico! 1951.

Experimental Cinema. 1930-1934 (all published).

Feldman, Joseph and Harry. Dynamics of the Film. 1952.

Film Daily Yearbook of Motion Pictures. Microfilm, 18 reels, 35 mm. 1918-1969.

Film Daily Yearbook of Motion Pictures. 1970.

Film Daily Yearbook of Motion Pictures. (Wid's Year Book). 3 vols., 1918-1922.

The Film Index: A Bibliography. Vol. I: The Film as Art. 1941.

Film Society Programmes. 1925-1939 (all published).

Films: A Quarterly of Discussion and Analysis. Nos. 1-4, 1939-1940 (all published).

Flaherty, Frances Hubbard. The Odyssey of a Film-Maker: Robert Flaherty's Story. 1960.

General Bibliography of Motion Pictures, edited by Carl Vincent, Riccardo Redi, and Franco Venturini. 1953.

Hendricks, Gordon. Origins of the American Film. 1961-1966. New Introduction by Gordon Hendricks.

Hound and Horn: Essays on Cinema, 1928-1934. 1971.

Huff, Theodore. **Charlie Chaplin.** 1951.

Kahn, Gordon. **Hollywood on Trial.** 1948.

New York Times Film Reviews, 1913-1968. 1970.

Noble, Peter. **Hollywood Scapegoat: The Biography of Erich von Stroheim.** 1950.

Robson, E. W. and M. M. **The Film Answers Back.** 1939.

Seldes, Gilbert. **An Hour with the Movies and the Talkies.** 1929.

Weinberg, Herman G., editor. **Greed.** 1971.

Wollenberg, H. H. **Anatomy of the Film.** 1947.

Wright, Basil. **The Use of the Film.** 1948.

DISSERTATIONS ON FILM

Beaver, Frank Eugene. **Bosley Crowther: Social Critic of the Film, 1940-1967.** First publication, 1974.

Benderson, Albert Edward. **Critical Approaches to Federico Fellini's "8½".** First publication, 1974.

Cohen, Louis Harris. **The Cultural-Political Traditions and Developments of the Soviet Cinema: 1917-1972.** First publication, 1974.

Dart, Peter. **Pudovkin's Films and Film Theory.** First publication, 1974.

Facey, Paul W. **The Legion of Decency: A Sociological Analysis of the Emergence and Development of a Social Pressure Group.** First publication, 1974.

Karpf, Stephen L. **The Gangster Film: Emergence, Variation and Decay of a Genre, 1930-1940.** First publication, 1973.

Lounsbury, Myron O. **The Origins of American Film Criticism, 1909-1939.** First publication, 1973.

Lyons, Timothy James. **The Silent Partner: The History of the American Film Manufacturing Company, 1910-1921.** First publication, 1974.

McLaughlin, Robert. **Broadway and Hollywood: A History of Economic Interaction.** First publication, 1974.

North, Joseph H. **The Early Development of the Motion Picture, 1887-1909.** First publication, 1973.

Rimberg, John. **The Motion Picture in the Soviet Union, 1918-1952.** First publication, 1973.

Sands, Pierre N. **A Historical Study of the Academy of the Motion Picture Arts and Sciences (1927-1947).** First publication, 1973.

Wolfe, Glenn J. **Vachel Lindsay: The Poet as Film Theorist.** First publication, 1973.